How to Draw Faces and Portraits for Beginners

Learn to Draw Amazing and Realistic Faces One Step At A Time - Shading, Proportions, Eyes, Hair, Different Angles and Much More!

Leia Bloom

★ ★ ★ ★ ★

Thank you for buying our book!

If you find this guidebook fun and useful, we would be very grateful if you post a short review on Amazon! Your support does make a difference and we read every review personally.

If you would like to leave a review, just head on over to this book's Amazon page and click "Write a customer review."

Thank you for your support!

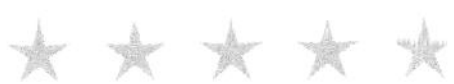

Contents

Introduction

The face is a complex form. Every individual has their own unique facial structure, from the shape, contours, texture, shade, proportions, and so on. Having this information in mind, most people might think that portraiture is an exceptional natural ability. Surely there's no way a typical person, with no background in drawing, could learn all those things in a short period of time, let alone in their lifetime. It is indeed true that portraiture can be challenging for beginners, but drawing is a skill, and skills can be acquired and mastered with time and practice. Let me share with you these three main ingredients to help to get started: Consistency, Patience, Enthusiasm. You will need to carry these ingredients with you throughout the book as I introduce you to portraiture.

In this book, I am going to help you learn all the basics, techniques, and different approaches you need to know in portraiture. We are going to cover everything, including the tools you'll need to master this skill and take it to heart. At the end of this book, I don't expect you to be walking down the gallery in an art museum as Leonardo da Vinci, but it is guaranteed that you will be miles away from thinking that portraiture is downright impossible. With enough practice, and an enthusiastic heart, you can even compete with those born with exceptional artistic abilities.

Tools You Will Need

PENCIL

GRAPHITE

One of the most common tools used in the art world is graphite. After all, almost every artwork starts with a sketch, right? Right. This tool is not just a typical pencil. I'm sure you've seen one that has designated marks with a letter and corresponding number. But what exactly do these marks mean?

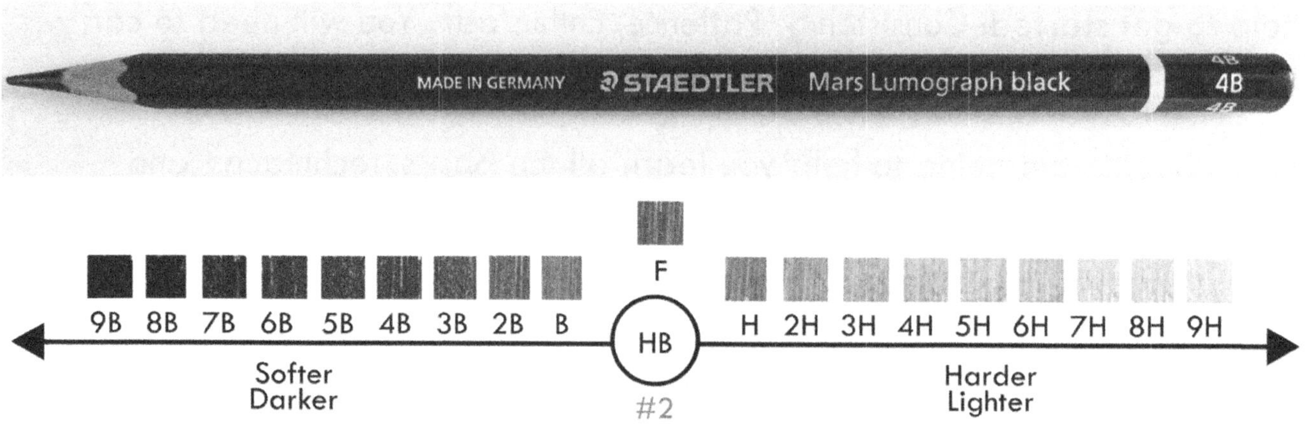

A common writing pencil is different to drawing pencils in that it only features a number. For instance, that pencil you've used almost your entire student life is usually marked with a number #2. Normally, that is also the required pencil number for those exams that require shading. That's because the #2 pencil is a standard writing pencil, which happens to have the corresponding softness as an "HB" drawing pencil.

H stands for Hard and features hard graphite, meaning that H pencils are lighter. B stands for Black or Blackness, which features soft graphite, meaning B pencils are darker. HB pencils fall in the middle of the scale, which, as mentioned earlier, is equivalent to a standard #2 writing pencil. For drawings, it is still reasonably categorized as hard. Meanwhile, F stands for Fine, which features a hard graphite that is very firm and is easy to keep sharp.

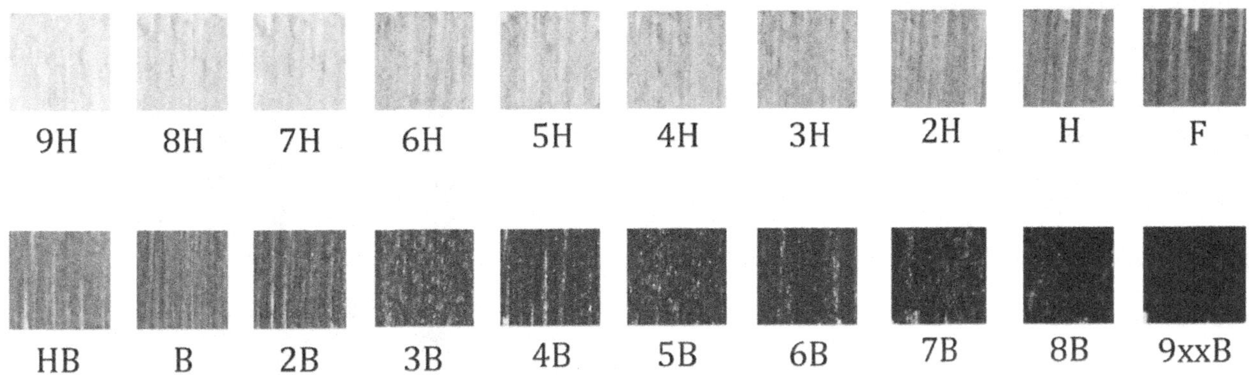

H pencils produce much lighter marks regardless of the pressure you apply when using them. The higher the number, the harder and lighter the pencil will be, so keep that in mind. Generally, H grades are commonly used for the initial sketch and are also ideal for light and precise strokes for a technical drawing.

B pencils are the opposite of H pencils; the higher the number, the softer and darker they are as you apply pressure. This makes them suitable for expressive and dramatic sketches and drawings. You can modify the darkness and line weight of your strokes by simply adjusting the amount of pressure you use. These are the pencils that you will need for creating shades and contrasts.

F pencils are almost as same as the HB, but slightly harder. This means they can be sharpened to an even finer point. An F pencil is perfect for a more precise stroke.

Remember, there is no need to have all these different grades of graphite pencils. Having a couple of lights and darks is enough for beginners or even for someone who's already an expert in drawing. If you're not certain which number to choose or use, here's my suggestion for beginners in portraiture: HB and F are a must-have. These are for light sketching. 4B and 6B are for shading and creating value and contrast. You may also choose your pencils two grades apart and try experimenting with them until you find the ones that fit your preferences.

Woodless Graphite Pencils

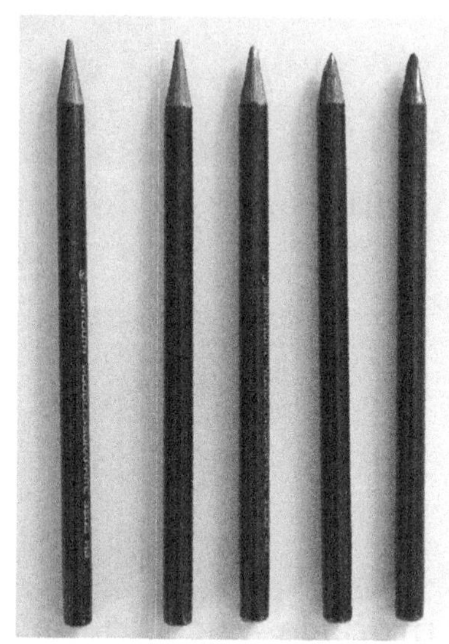

These are woodless pencils. They are also graphite pencils and are great if you don't enjoy sharpening. The only disadvantage is that they're brittle on account of having no wooden casing.

Charcoal Pencils

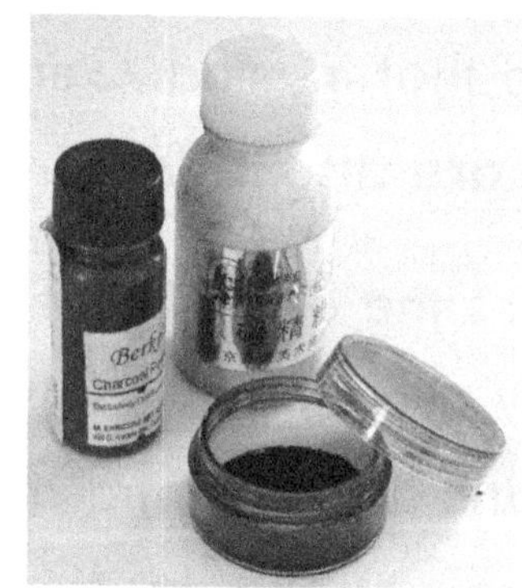

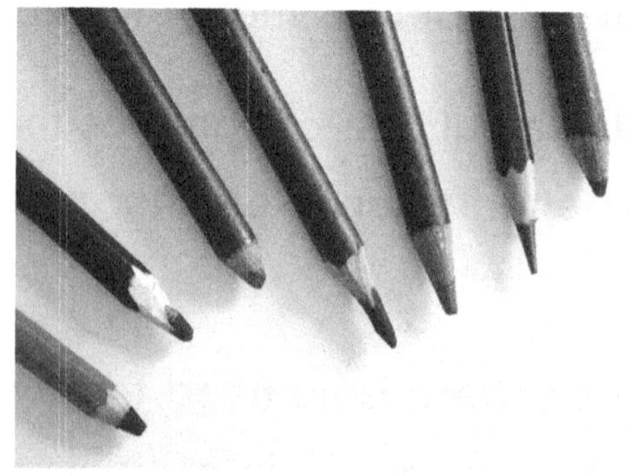

Charcoal is famous in portraiture. It's the kind of medium that can be used in an endless variety of ways. Thanks to its versatility, you can go from super soft and smooth to expressive and raw with a lot of texture. The concept of charcoal is just the same as graphite; it also has grades, but only three types. They are commonly referred to as Soft (B), Medium (HB), and Hard (H). There's no rule, really. It's up to your hands on how you'd like to make use of these grades. If you'd prefer to use just one grade for the entire drawing, then so be it. Keep in mind, though, that charcoal grades will be darker than graphite with the same grade. The advantage of charcoal is that it produces a richer, darker value than can be achieved in graphite. Charcoal also comes in matte finish when applied on paper, unlike graphite, which produces a shinier outcome.

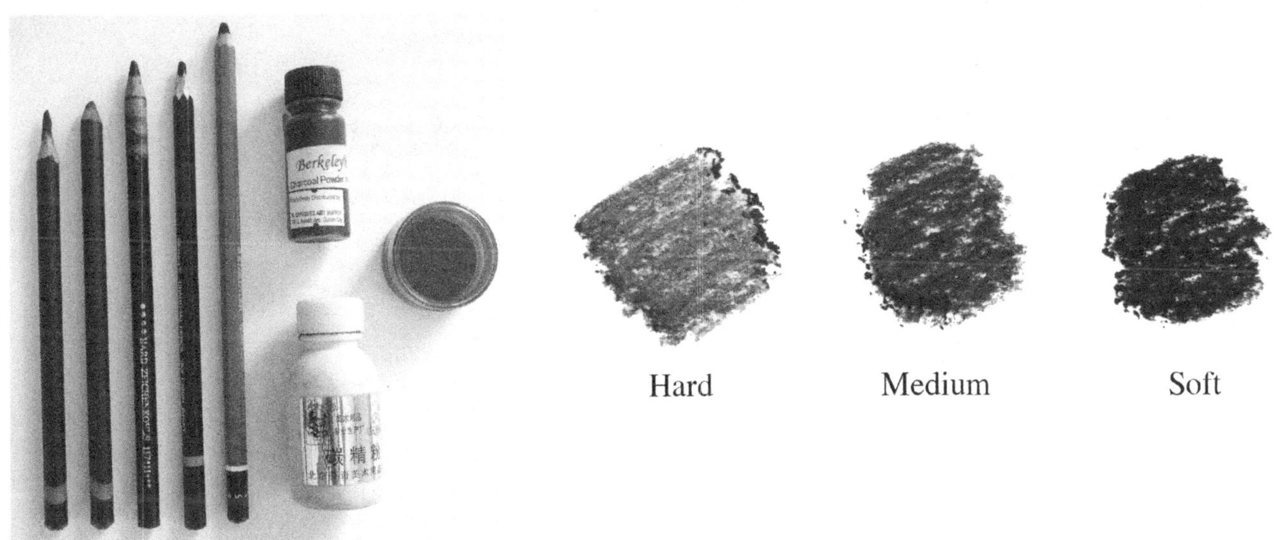

With soft charcoal, you get the softest texture, and it offers a rich, black color. Its versatility makes it the best grade when working with skin texture and hair in portraiture. In short, it is the primary tool for shading, and because of its softness, it can be easily lifted with a kneaded eraser. It can also be worked and reworked until the final value is achieved.

Medium charcoal, being the middle grade, is frequently used in drawing and sketching. It is great when working with mid-tone values. You get to manage the lighter and darker tone, which is great when it comes to detailing hair and the subtle outline of facial features.

Hard charcoal produces a lighter tone, and because it is firmer than the rest, it works well in fine areas. In portraiture, this type of grade is useful when it comes to intricate details, especially facial features. Also, hard charcoal doesn't erase easily, making it ideal for fine details.

Mechanical Pencil

Mechanical pencils are handy if you plan to bring your sketchbook along with you. These are pencil devices that can be refilled with graphite sticks, which are commonly available with grades 2B and HB. These pencils create constant lines because they don't need to be sharpened. They also provide the fastest way to produce a sketch.

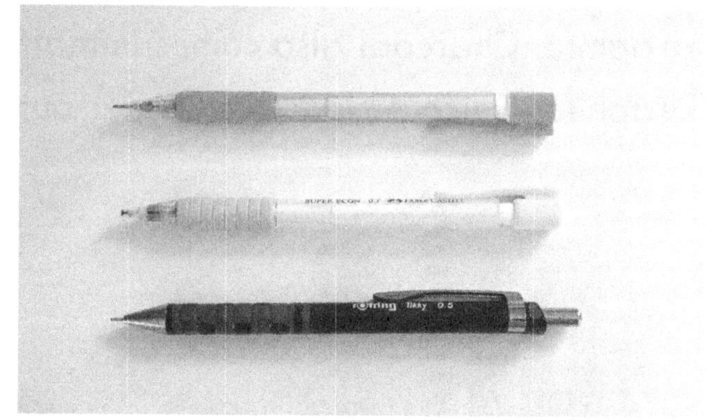

ERASERS

In portraiture, erasers are common tools for emphasizing highlights. Here are the different types of erasers and how to utilize their functions when drawing faces.

Rubber / Vinyl / Gum Erasers

These are standard erasers for erasing unnecessary pencil marks. When using them, make sure not to overdo it, as they might damage the surface of the paper. They also come in the form of a mechanical type, which resembles the concept of a mechanical pencil, and can be refilled with an eraser stick.

Kneaded Erasers

This is the primary type of eraser that graphite and charcoal artist use. It can be shaped and molded like a clay and easily picks up the graphite or charcoal without damaging the surface of the paper at all. It does not leave crumbs like a standard eraser. This eraser doesn't exactly erase marks but rather lightens them or makes them look soft, which is why it's a great tool for adding highlights to a face. The ideal way of using it is not to rub, but to press, rotate, and pull it away from the surface. You also need to "knead" it from time to time as a way of cleaning it.

Battery Operated Eraser

A battery-operated eraser is almost the same concept as a mechanical pencil. The eraser sticks are refillable, only this time it is battery operated. This type of eraser is strong enough to rub out the darkest pencil marks without completely damaging the surface. However, this only works with small details that you accidentally marked, for instance. It is also a great tool for producing hair strands and fine highlights.

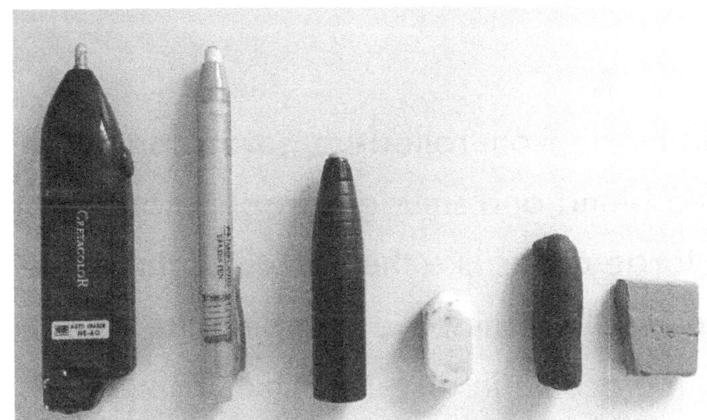

SHARPENERS

Sharpeners depend on the user's preference. However, I am going to share which sharpener is best for a specific type of pencil. As for graphite, you can use a typical sharpener. There are artist grade sharpeners available, but those are not as important for beginners. For charcoal pencils, since they're brittle and typical sharpeners are too rough, we normally use a knife/cutter. This way, you can also modify its shape to a certain angle, especially when you are using it for shading soft areas like the skin.

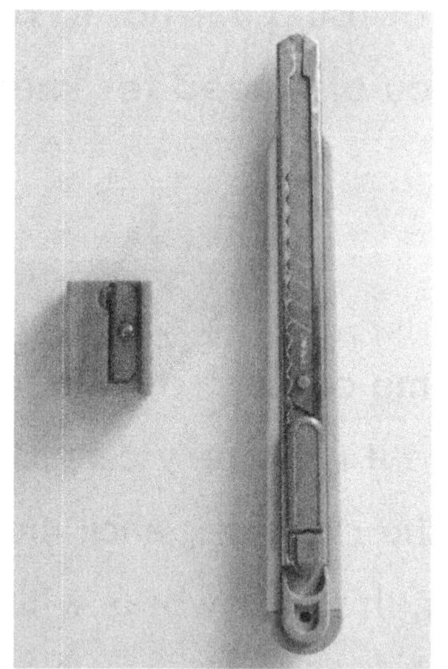

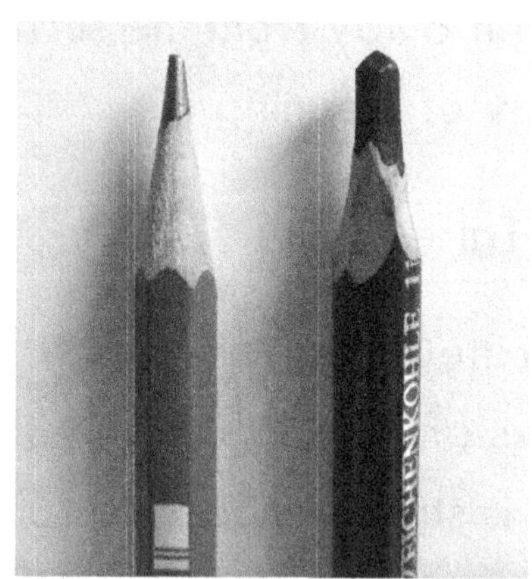

BLENDING TOOLS

Blending Stump

These are rigid sticks made from rolled-up, soft paper and pointed at each end. They are used to blend and smudge graphite and charcoal. These work well when blending large areas like the skin using the angled side, and the pointed parts are for small details, like blending the inner corner of the eye, lips, nose, and ears. They come in different sizes as well. For beginners, I recommend using a big and a small one first, and, as you go along, you can buy different sizes to experiment and find out which works best for you.

Tortillon

A lot of people confuse blending stumps with tortillon. Tortillons are also made of a tightly rolled paper but only with one point at the end. These are ideal for blending small areas, and we recommend using them at an angle to keep the pointed tip intact. Since tortillons aren't made with the same soft paper as blending stumps, it is difficult to maintain a consistent tone. However, they are great for blending even tighter spaces, where a high level of precision is required. I recommend having both paper blenders!

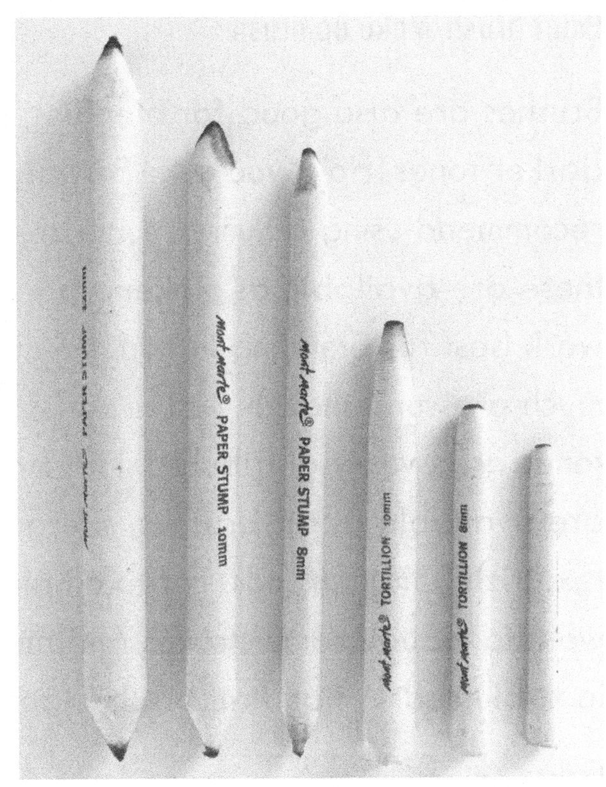

ALTERNATIVES TO BLENDING TOOLS

Tissue

Yes, that's right, paper towels or facial tissues work great for light or midtones. Dark graphite and charcoal will just transfer and spread on the surface, so tissues are not ideal for blending darker values. They are great, however, for blending the midtones in the skin and hair.

Q-Tip/Cotton swab

Q-Tips are a great alternative to blending stumps. Using their fine cotton ends, you can work on small areas that require blending. The only disadvantage is that they wear out quickly and are not good for long-term use. However, they are inexpensive and available in drugstores or supermarkets, so you can replace them instantly.

Paint brush/Make up brush

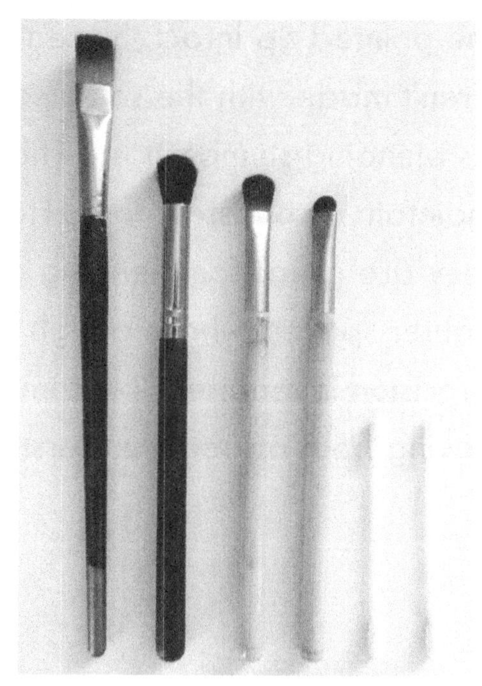

Brushes are also good for blending light and darker tones. How, you ask? For large areas, we recommend using a fluffy round brush. Normally, these are available as makeup brushes. They work best for blending in skin. Do not apply too much pressure, though. Just make sure that the tones are evenly distributed. Flat brushes, which are available as art brushes, are great for texturizing hair strands. For example, you may want to include some strokes and make them look blurred. A flat, firm brush is good for this.

In blending, never use your finger. Our fingers contain oils that will just make the paper look greasy and dirty. It will also be hard to erase. If you insist upon using your finger because you feel it gives you greater control, make sure to wrap it up with a tissue.

PAPERS

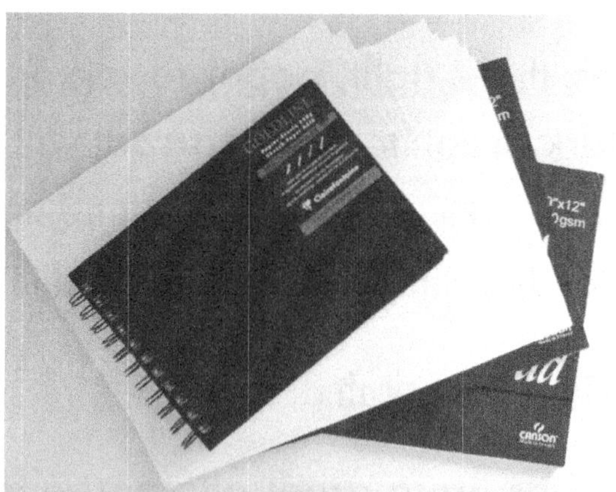

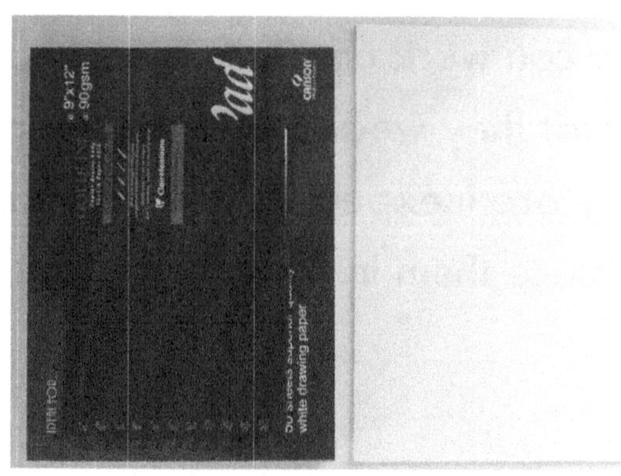

When it comes to charcoal/graphite portraiture, it is important to choose high-quality paper. For beginners, my advice would be to choose the paper that you're most comfortable with. An artist grade paper is not yet necessary at this stage, but if you're determined enough, it won't pose a problem.
Just try experimenting on different types of paper until you find your personal preference. Let's start with understanding the qualities of paper

Size

The size of your paper is not much of an issue, be it a small sketchpad, A3 size, paper boards or even a journal sketchpad. There are pros and cons to each, though. When using a small sketchpad for portraiture, it might be difficult for you to include all the details, as intricate details would require a good amount of focus. Additionally, chances are you might not be able to draw them accurately. However, the pros are that small sketchpads are handy and can be brought anywhere, which is ideal if you're planning on doing a plein air study.

Texture

Choosing the right kind of texture for your drawing will depend on your style. If you're more of a rough sketcher and not concerned with fine, intricate details, then either a rough or smooth paper will do. If you're more into fine, realistic drawing, on the other hand, then I recommend using a smooth, velvety surface. These come in papers and boards.

Weight

"90gsm, 100gsm, 200gs, 300gsm" – I'm sure you've encountered one of these written on papers or a sketchpad. What do they mean? GSM stands for Grams per Square Meter. The higher the GSM number, the heavier and thicker the paper. As a beginner in portraiture, the standard 90gsm sketchpad is good for practice. Eventually, when you get better and plan on putting your artworks in a frame, I suggest you go for 300gsm, as this will result in less tearing or crumpling.

It's a good idea to spend time experimenting and studying charcoal on different paper types. Before you even know it, you'll probably find a surface you love to work on. For now, grab that sketchpad you recently bought!

Coating

In the art world, there's this thing we call 'fixative spray'. Although these sprays are optional, they are a great tool for preserving your artwork, especially when you're working with a dry medium that is prone to smudging. For beginners, while you are still in practice, I recommend not using these sprays for now, as they're quite expensive, especially the good quality ones.

However, if you're eager to try the sprays out, make sure to read the instructions carefully. If you overdo the spray, it may result in damage to your drawing, and we don't want that. Try spraying it out on a piece of paper first, because the distance you must spray varies depending on the brand of the paper. Allow it to dry and evaluate whether you need a second coating. Inspect it first carefully before giving it another spray. The maximum suggested coating is 3, although normally a 2nd coat shows great results.

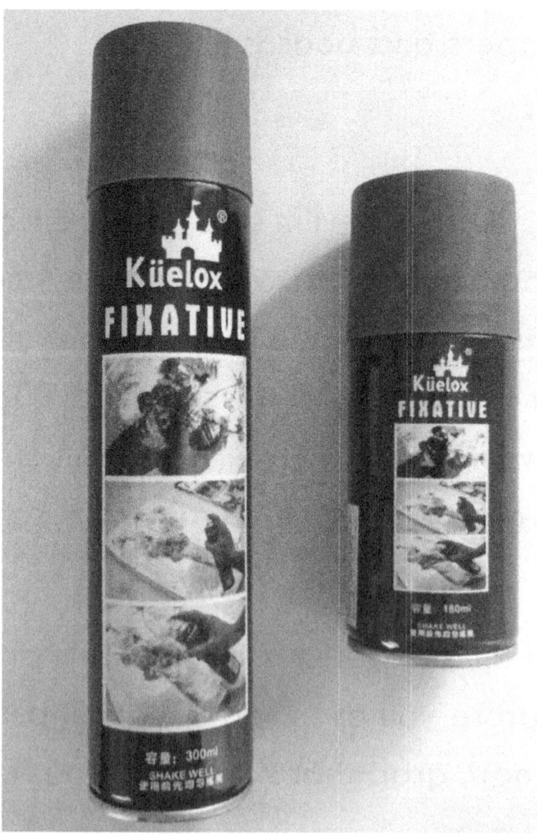

Different Shading Techniques

Shading is an important aspect when it comes to drawing, especially in portraiture. Shading is the process of building those values in a drawing to produce the illusion of light, shadows, form, and space. Properly executed shading can make a drawing appear three-dimensional. I am going to teach you the four basic techniques in shading to level up your game.

Hatching

The hatching technique is the simplest of all shading techniques, and there are 3 ways to do it. It can be done vertically, horizontally, or diagonally all throughout or a mix of these 3. For beginners, it is best to use one direction first. Using these 3 directions all at once is possible, but if not done well, it will look messy. When doing the hatch, make sure that your hands are relaxed so the strokes are smooth rather than crooked.

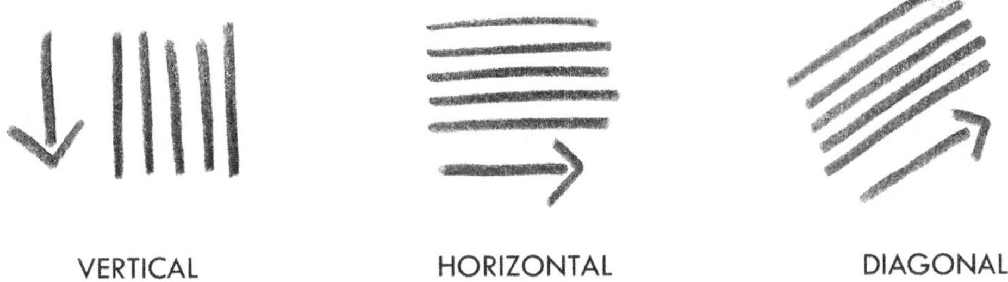

VERTICAL HORIZONTAL DIAGONAL

This is how it's supposed to look when you do the strokes for hatching. For practice, try doing hatches on boxes repeatedly until you get the hang of it. Here's a leaf shape, for example. Observe how this leaf shape was shaded using hatching, leaving the

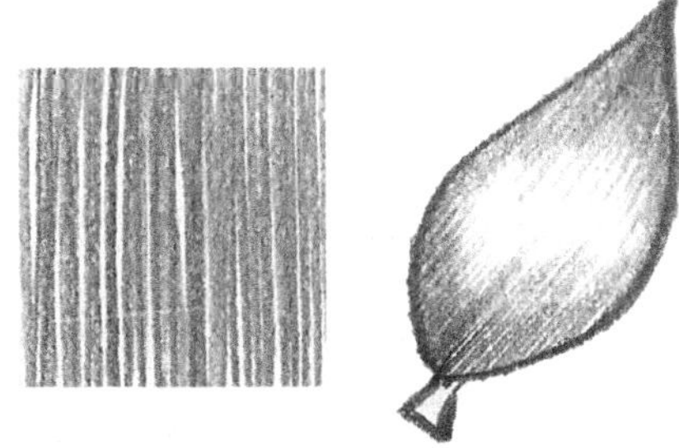

center blank to create an illusion of highlights. When it comes to values, specifically when doing the shadows, do two to three layers of hatch. For midtones, a single layer is enough.

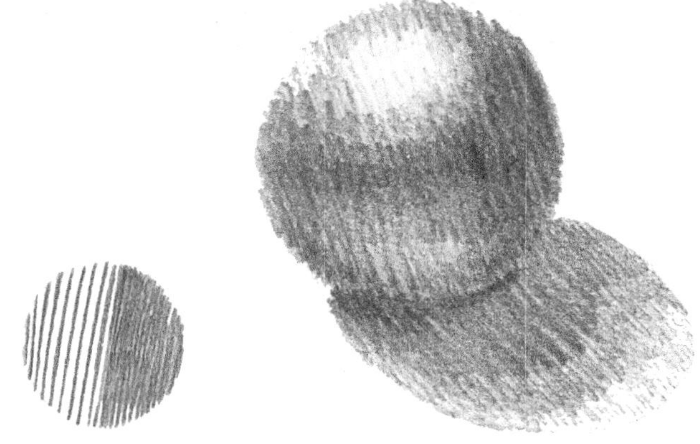

Cross hatching

Cross hatching is basically a combination of two diagonal lines in opposite directions. Combining them together at their intersection makes a "cross" pattern. It is important when you cross hatch that the lines are at a uniform angle throughout the whole sketch.

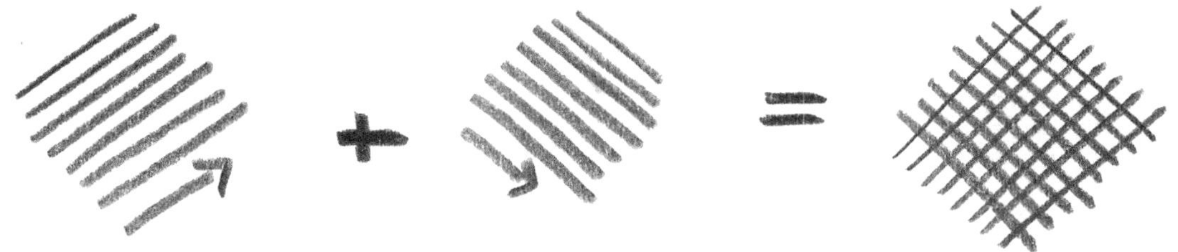

For practice, do cross hatching on different shapes so you can learn to have more control over the edges. When you only practice doing hatchings on a box, your hands will automatically know where to land, and that would not be helpful when you're doing a sketch with lots of curved edges, for instance, a portrait.

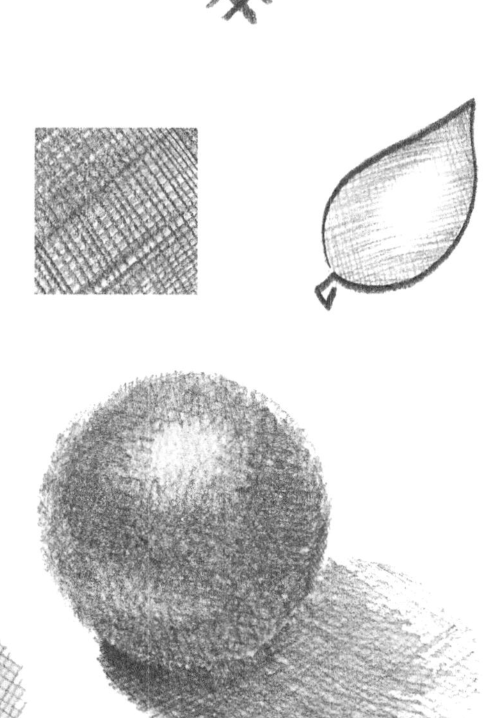

Scribbling/Circulism

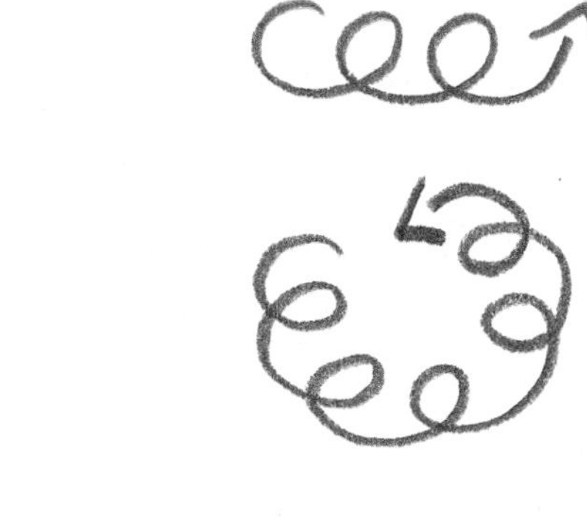

Scribbling can be done in two ways. First, you can do loops in a linear direction. This is most useful when the shape of the object you're shading has uniform edges. The second way is to do loops in circular direction. This is most useful when you're shading a very complicated shape and edges. It's also most effective when this particular shading technique is blended. It creates a smooth outcome.

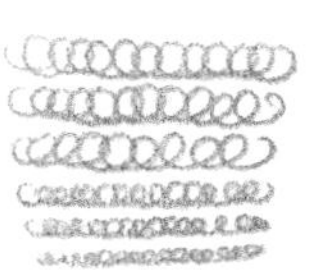

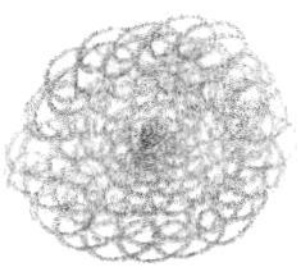

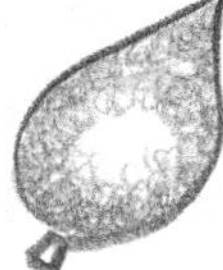

This is an example of circulism in linear loops. Remember, smaller and tighter loops mean that the area you're shading is the darkest or most shadowed. Bigger and wider loops represent midtones and highlights. That is how you use circulism in values.

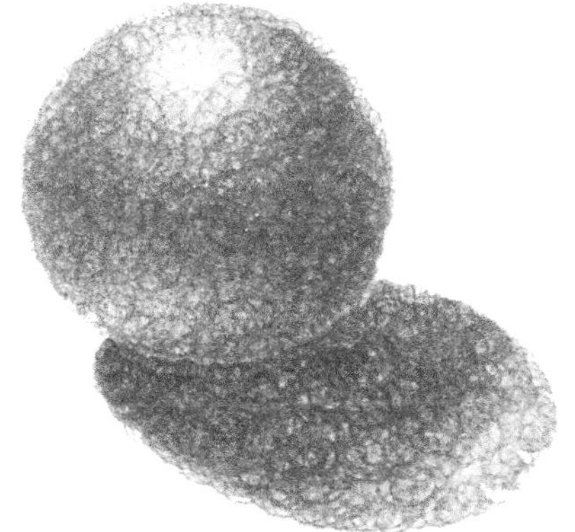

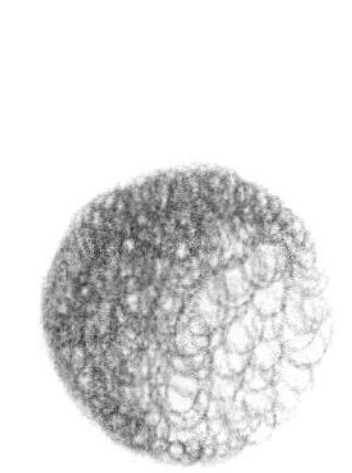

Stippling

Stippling is basically when you dab your pencil repeatedly on your drawing surface to produce dots. This may take patience, but the outcome, when done well, comes out smooth. This can be done using any grades of pencil according to your preference. Make sure when doing this that you don't

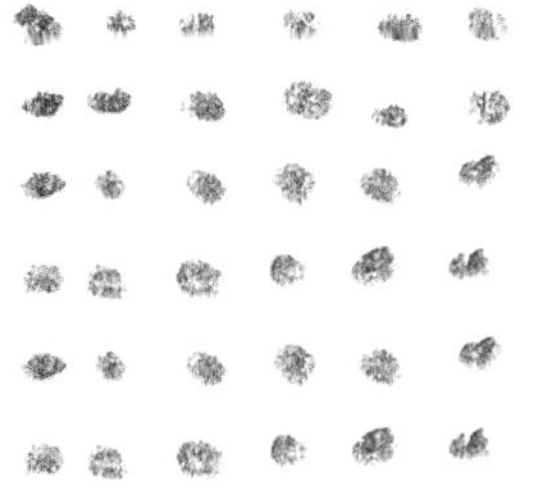

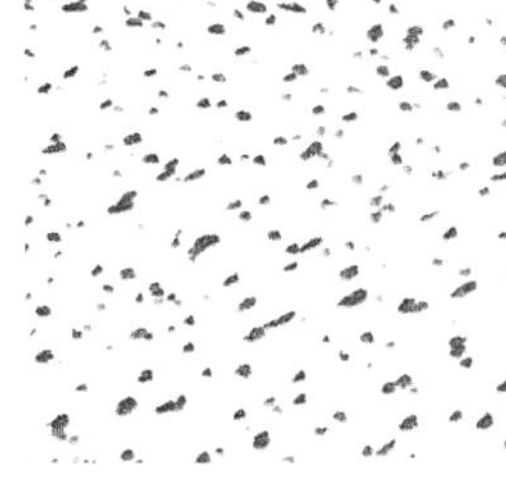

dab it too hard, as you might damage the surface. This technique is an “as is” shading technique. This means it cannot be blended like the previous techniques we discussed.

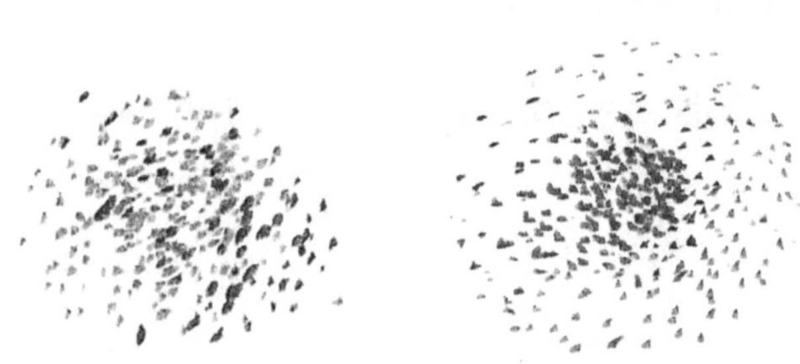

In stippling, when you portray a highlighted area, you need to simply scatter the dots. Make sure they are away from each other. For shadow, compress them as much as possible to make a darker area. Again, this requires lots of patience! But the outcome will amaze you! See for yourself!

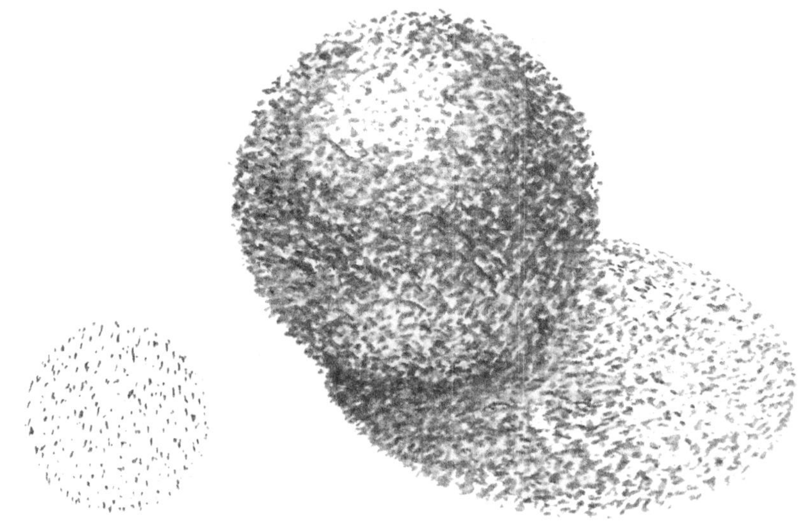

Understanding Light

Ever wonder why portraiture is such a challenging subject? Be it charcoal, graphite, watercolor, acrylic, oil, or any other mediums, it involves turning a 2-dimensional sketch into a 3-dimensional one. We create the illusion of a realistic picture.

In this topic, you are going to learn about how light works, how shadow forms, and the importance of value and contrast. All these contribute to an ordinary drawing becoming extraordinary. When you keep these basics in mind, you will make your artworks more realistic.

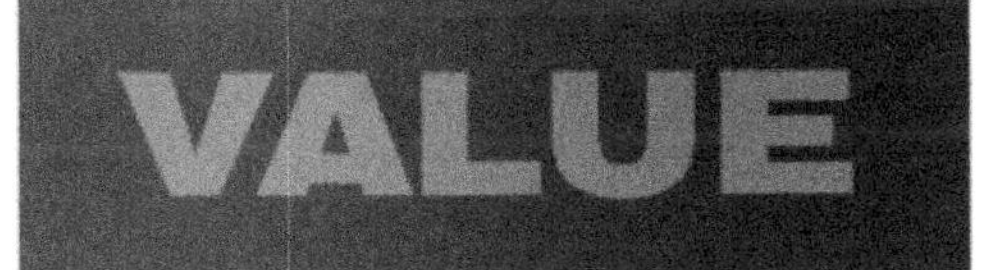

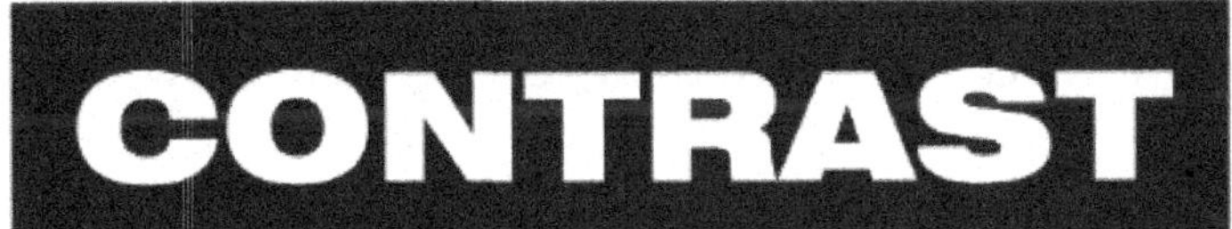

Value deals with how light or dark a given color and hue can be. Values can be understood as a gradient, from dark to light. Drawing and painting is about seeing. Therefore, the reason we see and understand objects based on how light and dark they are is because of value. That is how important value is in art. In order to draw or paint in a way that produces an illusion of what we normally see, we must completely understand light and how it is reflected on surfaces. The key to the illusion of light is value.

Contrast, on the other hand, deals with the difference between elements, such as light and dark, opposite hues on the color wheel, texture, and size. It can be subtle or extreme. However, in portraiture, we are mostly concerned with the contrast that is created from changes in value.

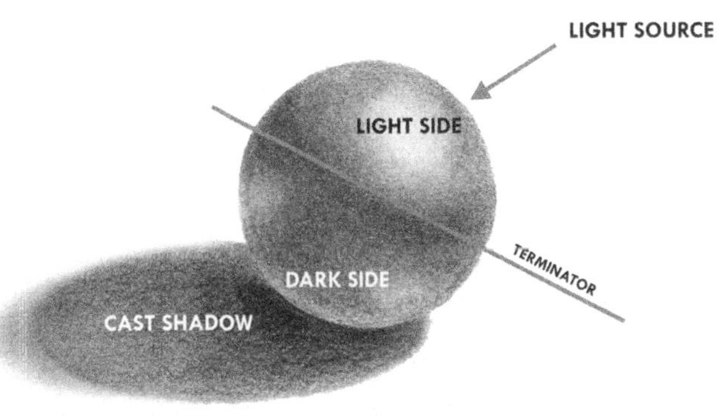

Light Source and Shadows

Light in drawing does not only refer to an artificial light. It can be the sun, the moon, or a light through a window. When light is projected onto your subject, it creates lights, darks, and casts shadows. When there are several light sources on a certain object or figure, light and dark tones vary and are less predictable. Don't fret though; studying light in drawing can be achieved through observation and constant practice.

THREE KINDS OF SHADOWS

There are three kinds of shadows that occur when a single light shines on an object: a form shadow, a cast shadow, and an occlusion shadow.

Cast shadow appears when an object or form blocks light from reaching the surface of another object. Depending on the intensity of the light source, the edges of a cast shadow can appear soft or hard. For instance, in a direct light source, the edges may appear hard, while in a diffused light source, they may appear soft and cloudy.

Occlusion shadow, on the other hand, is immediately below the object. It is usually the darkest area which is least affected by reflected light.

Form shadow, also called 'core shadow', is the dark area that appears after the terminator. It has softer and less-defined edges than a cast shadow. Normally, form shadows are subtle shadows that are essential for creating the illusion of volume, mass, and depth.

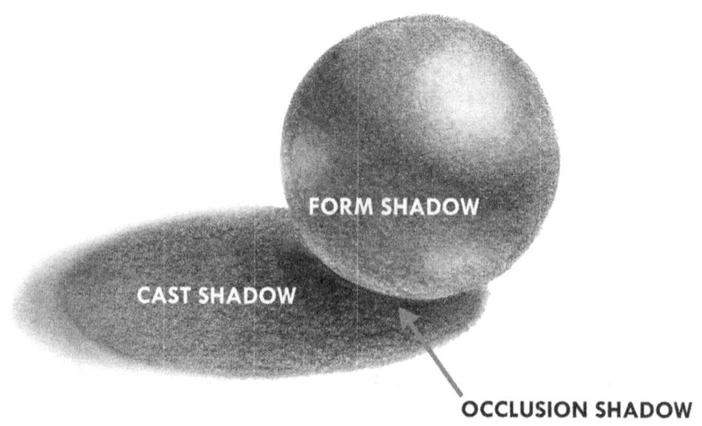

The Dark Side in Three Parts

SHADOW EDGE OR CORE SHADOW

Shadow edge is the darkest value on the dark side where the light is blocked from the light source. It is also commonly referred to as the 'terminator', which means the transition zone. It usually appears as an edge, a line, or a plane which doesn't reach direct light and reflective light.

DARK MIDDLE TONE

This is the blended part of the core shadow. Dark middle tones, however, are still darker than the middle tone in the light area. They may appear to have the same value, but they still have subtle differences. To know their difference, train your eyes into differentiating the two with any available source you have.

REFLECTED LIGHT

Reflected light occurs when light is reflected on an object from the surface where it sits. Say, for example, the object is sitting on a white surface. The light from that surface reflects onto the object and makes the shadow side lighter. The same is true when the surface is colored; its reflected light is the same color as the surface.

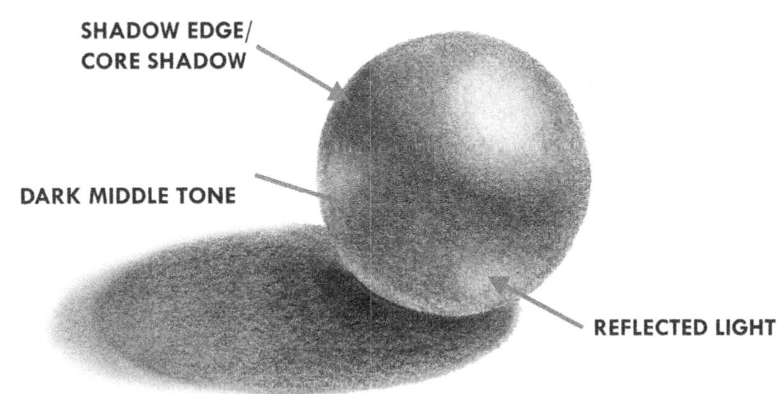

The Light Side in Two Parts

HIGHLIGHT

The highlight is the location on the object where the reflection of light is most intense. It will be the lightest part in the subject. Its appearance depends on the texture of the surface; it will appear shiny and defined on a glass and metallic surface, fuzzy and muted on textured surfaces, and very soft on matte surfaces.

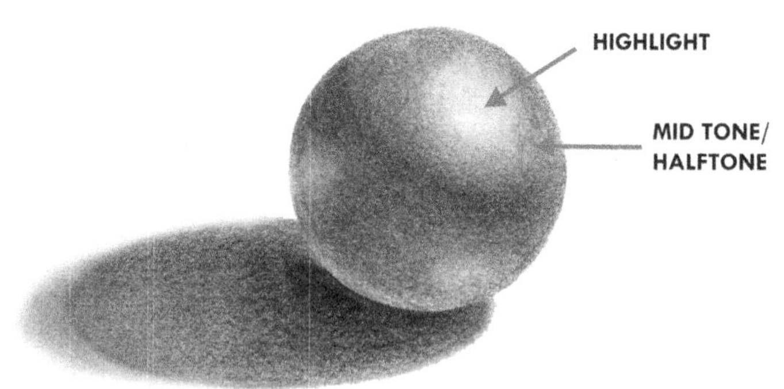

MIDTONES/HALFTONES/LIGHT MIDDLE TONE

These areas are not facing light directly. They are the darkest value on the light side but lighter than the core shadow. Normally, midtones are the actual color or value of the subject. These are the blended part of the core light.

The figure below shows how light sources affect the shape of the shadow cast upon an object.

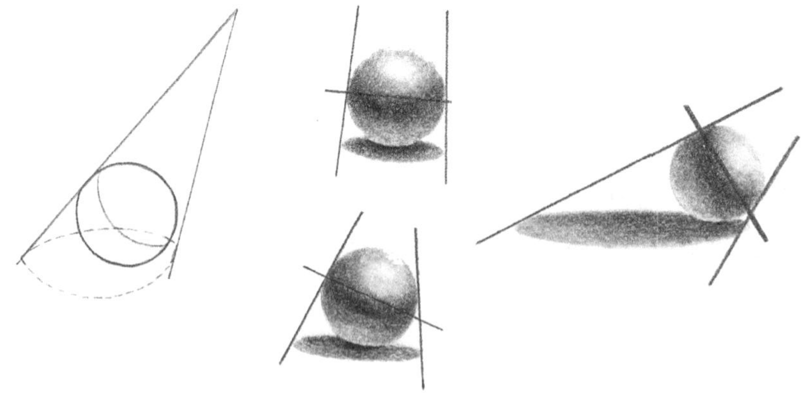

Here are some examples of different shapes and how light affects the value on them. For this figure, we can see a cylinder and a cone. Observe how the light source can modify their respective shadows.

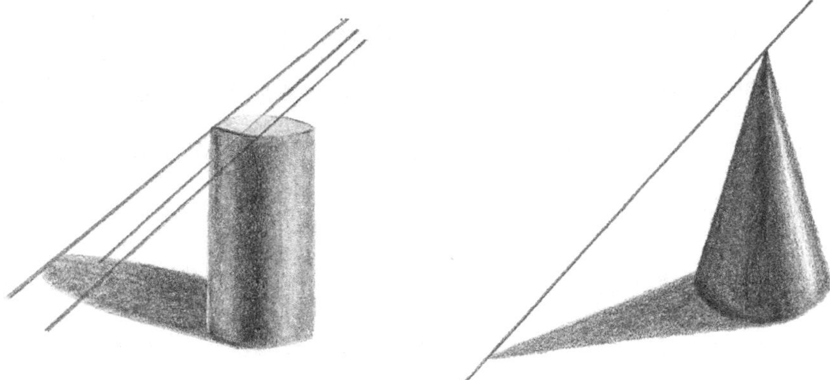

For objects with flat surfaces, like the cube below, the value stays consistent for each side without showing much gradient. Each side of the cube represents the highlight, midtone, and core shadow.

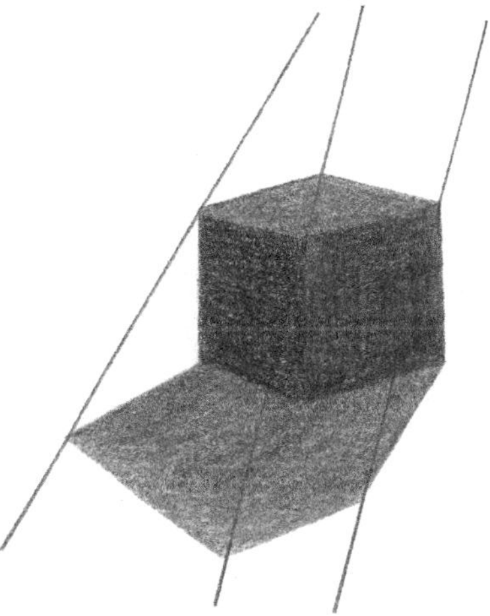

Once you get the hang of how light works, every drawing you create will appear realistic. Painting or drawing realistically isn't about focusing on lines and shapes; it's more about the form and edges. Once you have a clear understanding of how light and shadows behave, then you're already halfway there. Practice drawing a few basic forms first and, once you've mastered them, move on to irregular objects like fruits or any household items. Observe more carefully and train your vision to see the light that falls and the shadow that is cast. This requires a lot of patience, but the more you practice, the more you'll improve.

Drawing Accuracy

"Draw what you see." I'm sure we've all heard this phrase countless times already. It is the most acceptable advice because drawing is really about observation and translating your visions to paper. To improve your drawing skills, you must learn how to truly see the subjects that you draw. Therefore, you must know what to look for.

The techniques we are about to discuss are not the sole solution, but rather act as guides designed to improve your accuracy in drawing. Just like any other skill, constant practice is required to master them.

SIGHTING/MEASURING

This technique works best for on-the-spot drawing or drawing from life. While drawing from photographs is a necessity for artists, being able to draw what's in front of you without leaning on photographs is an invaluable skill.

Normally, we use tools for this technique. But don't fret; use any tool that works best for you. Usually, a pencil does the trick. Here's how it works:

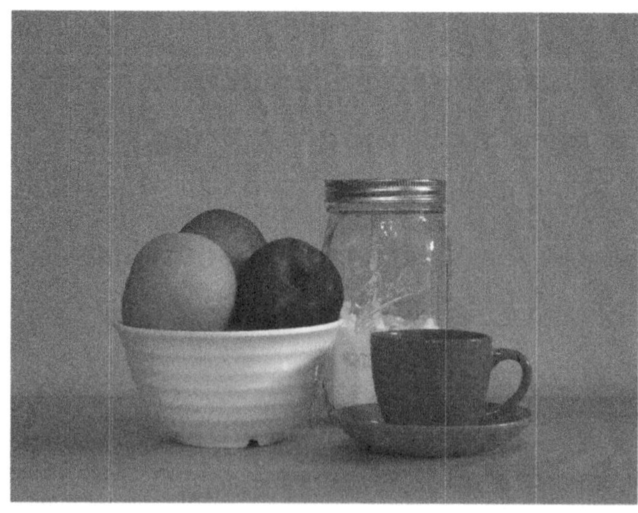

Make sure that you don't move your position during the whole process. Start by extending your arm out with your pencil towards your subject and make sure your arm is extended completely, without bending your elbow. Make sure your sight is level with your shoulders. Close your one eye when you try to do the measuring. Use the tip of the pencil to mark the edge of an object, either vertically or horizontally. Then, use your thumb to mark the other edge. Now you have the measurement of the object, you can record and compare this onto your drawing paper for your initial sketch. It doesn't have to be perfect yet. Just make sure the measurements and shapes are similar to what you see.

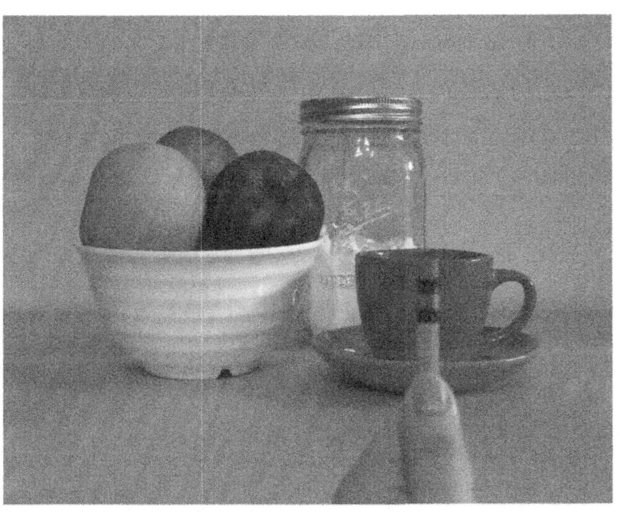

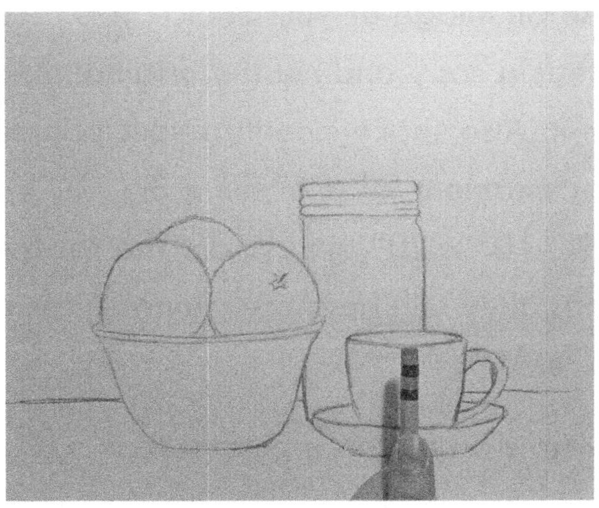

Try to measure all the objects in your subject in the same manner. Then, keep comparing your measurement to the relationship of each object in the scene.

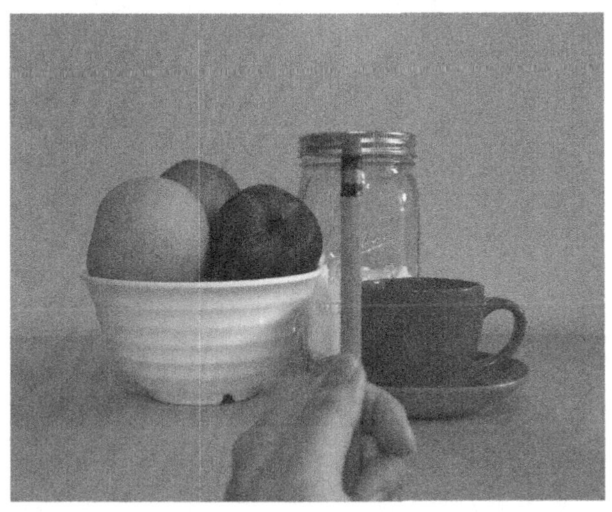

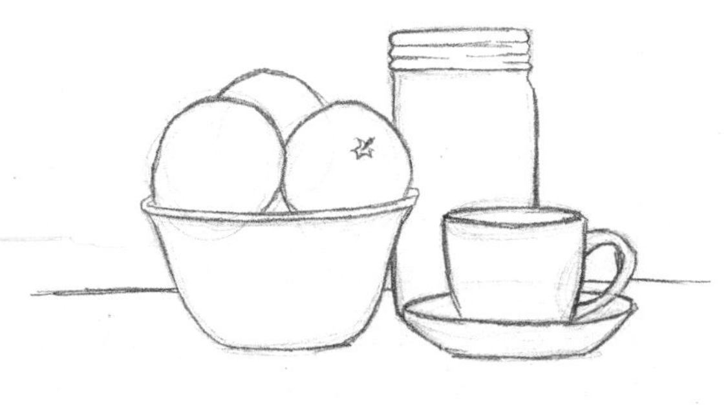

When you are done with the initial rough sketch, and you think it's almost accurate, you can do the final, clean sketch. Thereafter, you can finalize everything with whatever medium you plan to use.

GRID TECHNIQUE

Unlike the first technique, this one is used when your reference is a photo. This kind of approach is done by breaking the subject into small frames. This way, you'll get the drawing as accurate as possible. This is the kind of technique that works best for drawing portraiture.

Use an image of your choice. It is recommended that the photo you're going to use is a copy and not the original, because you are going to draw and write on it. Also, make sure that your printed photo's dimension is a whole number. For example, 6" x 6", 8" x 8", 10" x 10", 6" x 10", 5" x 9", 7" x 11", 8" x 12", 10" x 20", and so on. The reason for this is that when you draw the grid lines, they will be proportional in terms of measurement on all sides without excess.

Here is a reference picture that is 8" x 10" in size. As you can see, the grids that are drawn over the image are made of inch squares, and they are proportional on all sides.

Note: For this guide, the unit we used is in "inches" because it is the easiest way to measure and is commonly used. However, you can use the unit you're most comfortable with. Inches and centimeters are usually the common units.

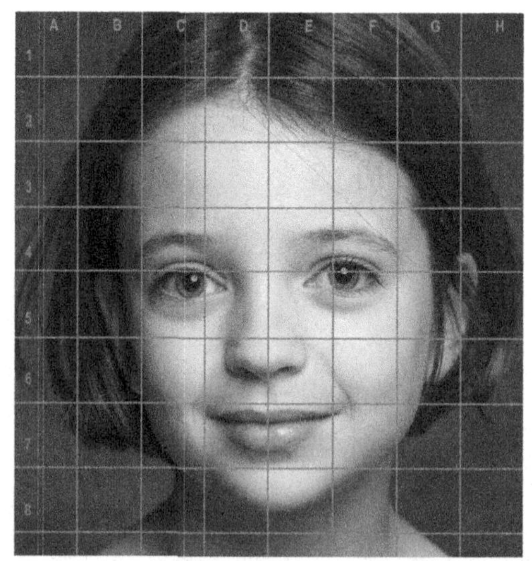

The picture below is an example where the dimensions are not in whole numbers. You can see that there will be excess unless you divide it well to make your grids equal, but that would be time consuming and very complex. The goal here is to simplify the drawing itself, so using the easiest way in this technique is essential.

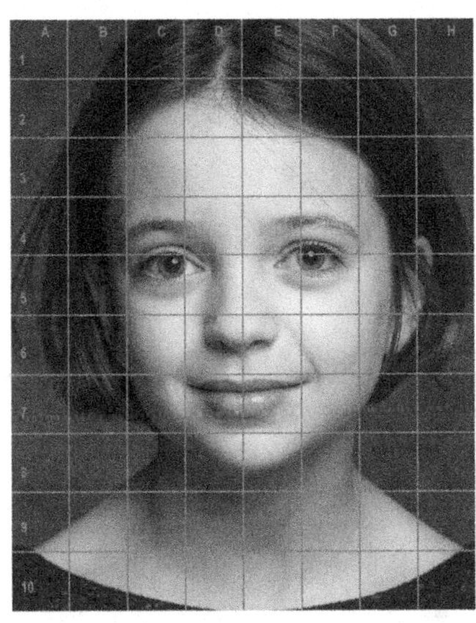
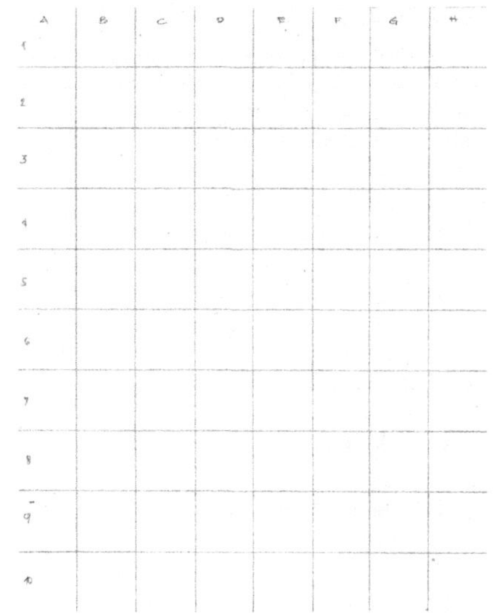

Now, make sure that your paper is the same size as your reference photo. Draw the grid in the same manner as the one you did on your photo. Make sure that you draw the grid on your paper lightly so that it can be easily erased later. Next, label the boxes horizontally and vertically. You can use letters, numbers, or both. When you label both your paper and the photo, you can check whether their grids match. If they do, you did it correctly.

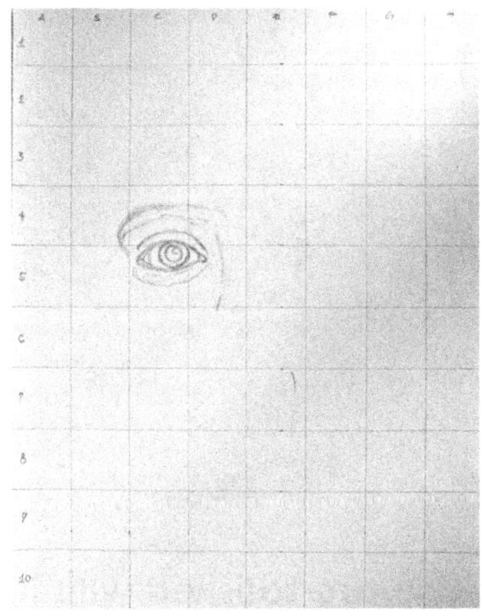

Now that everything is set, you can start drawing. Begin by drawing each section, one square at a time. Since the subject is simplified into sections, make sure to focus on each of the lines, shapes, and values in each square, rather than trying to think of the about the shape of what you are drawing.

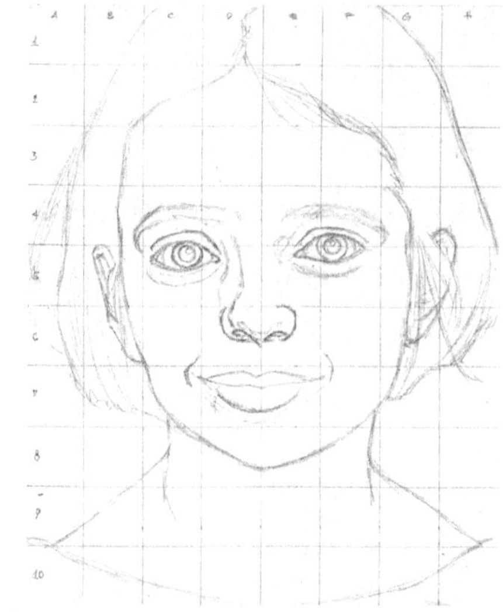

Take your time and fill each square slowly. Don't be afraid to rework each square if you feel they are not accurate enough. Have enough patience, and in no time, you will see that you've created an accurate drawing from a photo.

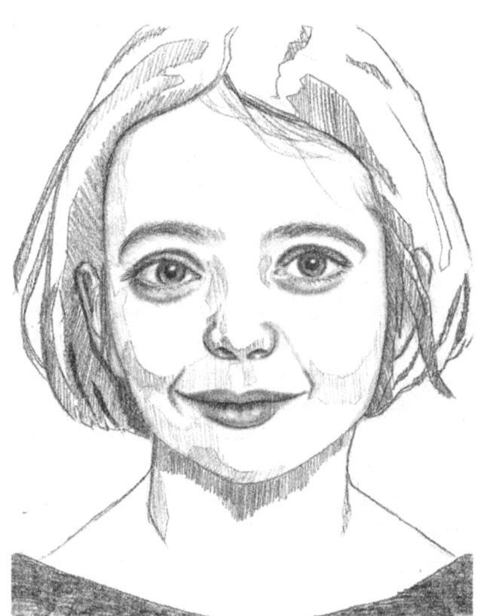

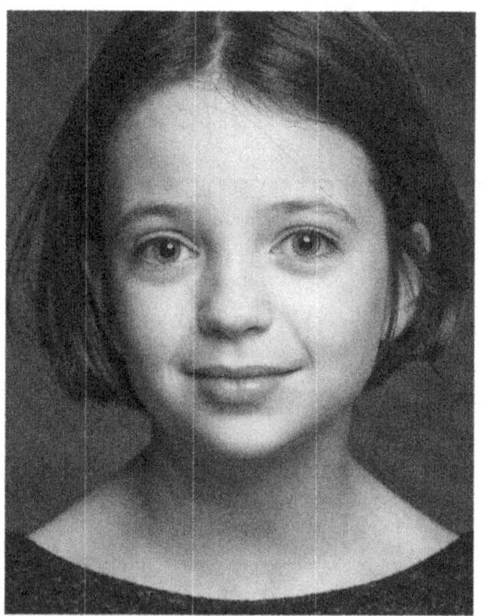

When you are satisfied with it, erase the grid lines without ruining the drawing. Finalize everything and there you have it: a proportional portrait drawing.

TRIANGULAR GRID TECHNIQUE

This is another version of the popular grid technique. This technique, though a bit complicated for a beginner, is preferred by many artists. Nevertheless, it's up to what works best for you, so try to give this a shot too.

Just like in the grid technique, you will need the same dimension on a reference photo and your drawing surface. To start drawing the triangles, divide the length and width of the photo and your paper. Next, draw a pair of vertical and horizontal lines crossing to the center and additionally, two diagonal lines from each corner. You will make eight triangles within the grid.

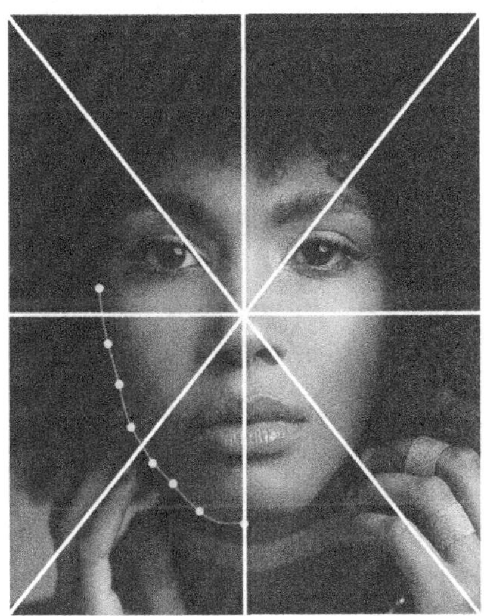

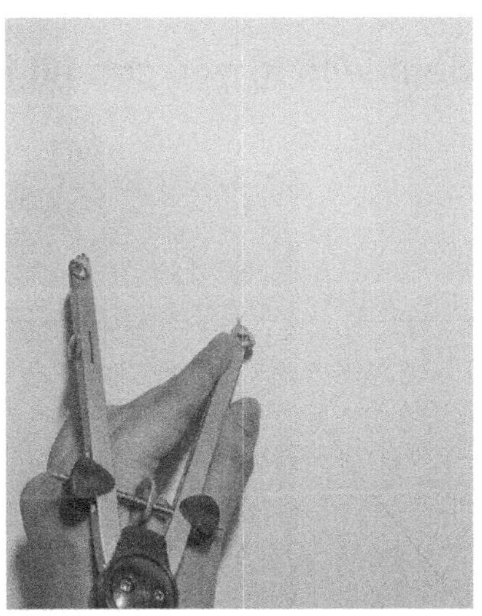

You will need a specific tool for this: a compass or a proportional divider. Use the end of your preferred tool as positioned in the center and the other end will mark the location of the edges or various references of your subject. This is almost like transferring the measurement directly from the photo to your paper. When you have all the important marks, use those to draw the contour lines of the subject, connecting the dots.

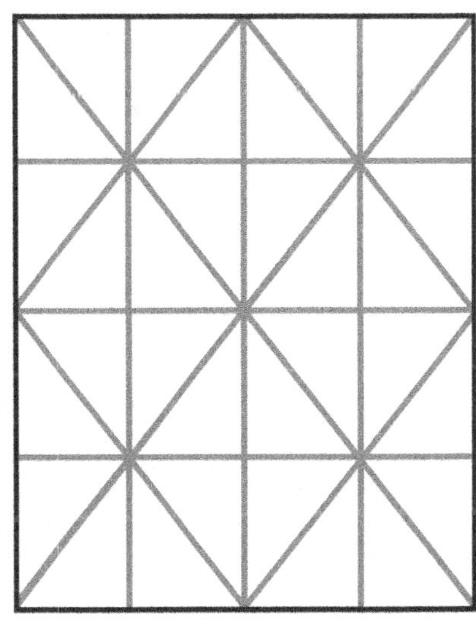

If you're having a hard time making it accurate because the lines of the triangles are too far from each other, you can always add more triangles like this.

IDENTIFYING BASIC SHAPES

Most of the time, objects can come in complex shapes and forms, making them hard to draw. No matter how complex they all look, there is an easy way to simplify them. This is done by breaking them into basic shapes. This technique is normally useful for either still life or with a reference photo. The first step is to take time to observe and study the relationships of those shapes in your subject before even attempting to draw. Once you've got it figured out, plot the shapes on your drawing surface. It's fine to draw them loosely, and as you become confident with it, you can fill in the details.

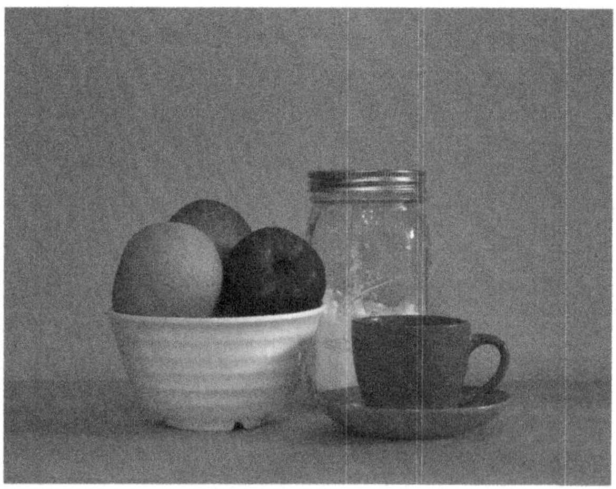

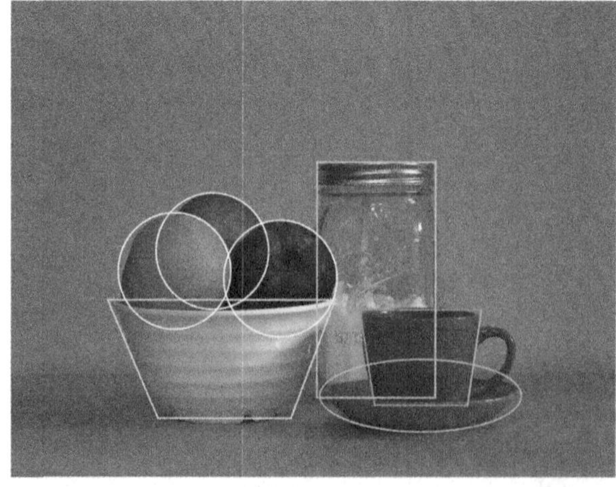

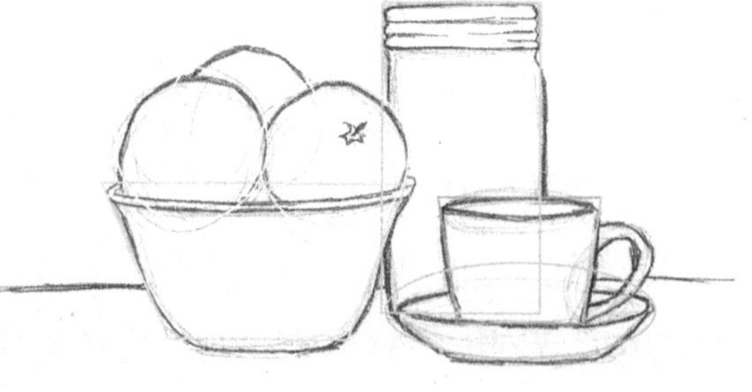

Let's take this reference photo as an example once again. The fruits are translated as circles, the jar into a rectangle, and so on. Remember that basic shapes aren't limited to circles, squares, and rectangles. You can also make use of uncommon shapes like a trapezoid, which can help you get the shape of certain objects as accurate as possible.

BASIC PROPORTIONS

Every face is unique, and we all know that for sure. However, typical facial proportions do exist. Whether you are drawing from imagination or with a reference, you can use this handy technique. There are two ways to do this.

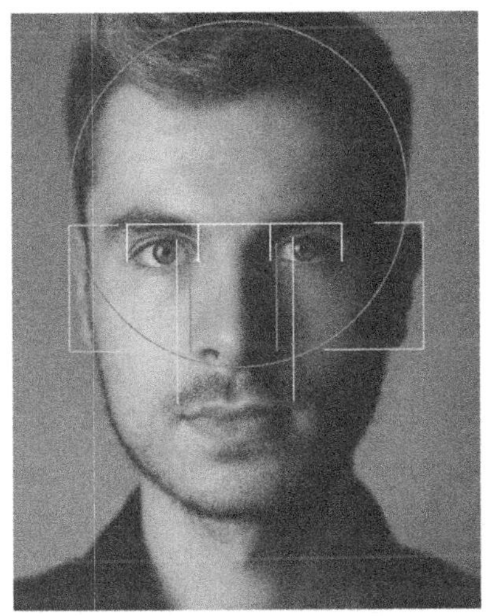
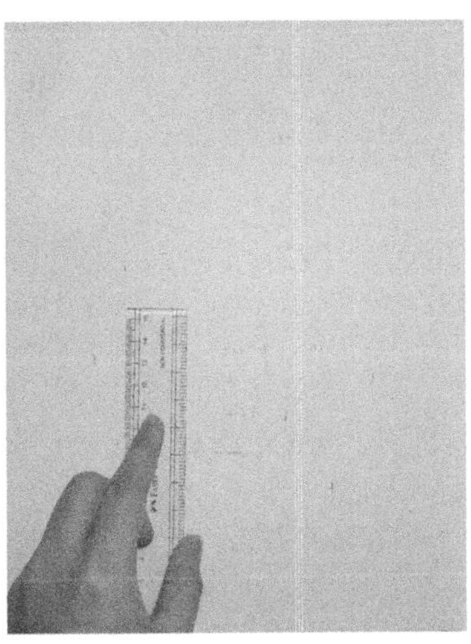

First, you can study the basic facial proportions. The distance between the eyes is usually equal to the horizontal length of one eye. The end of the lips is usually aligned with the eyeball, the edge of the nose is usually aligned with the end of the tear duct, and so on. This may not result in the most accuracy as a beginner, but it is a helpful tool for artists. As with all techniques, it comes with practice.

The second way to do this is with a reference photo. Make sure that the size of the drawing you want is the same as your reference. For this technique, you'll need a ruler. Basically, you are just going to transfer the measurement from your reference to your paper. It is somewhat similar to the sighting technique, but this one results in the most accurate measurements. Simply plot the marks of your measurements onto your paper, and when you think it's good enough, fill in the details.

These are the most common techniques for making the proportions of your drawing accurate. You don't have to choose only one to master, as these are all helpful at some point depending on your subject. Remember that, above all, observation will always be the first step in all the techniques presented. So, learn the art of observation; it's an artist's secret.

Line Weight

Line quality or line weight is essential in art, especially in drawing. It commonly defines the edges of an object. Drawing a line by using only a single width makes your object monotonous, boring, and cartoony. It is necessary to add a variety of lines in terms of depth to make the subject more appealing. Incorporating depth and weight of line is what makes a drawing look more realistic. This is an essential technique in portraiture.

THICK AND THIN LINES

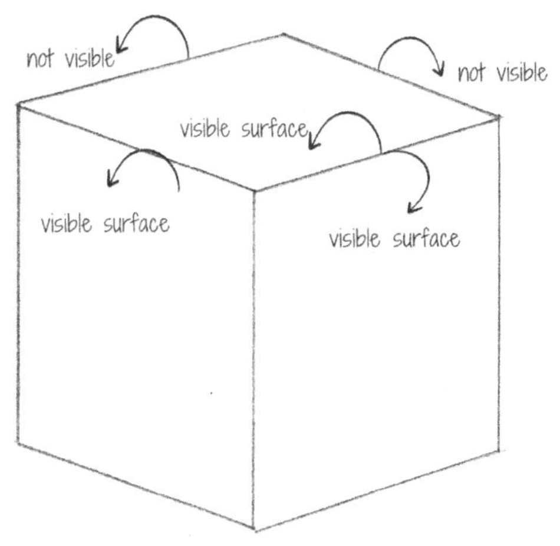

Let's start off with identifying when and where we should put thick and thin lines respectively. We'll use the example of a cube to make the explanation more understandable. If two surfaces are together or are visible, and you can see the edge that is created by them, then that edge is going to be the "thin line."

However, when only one surface is visible, that edge is going to be the "thick line."

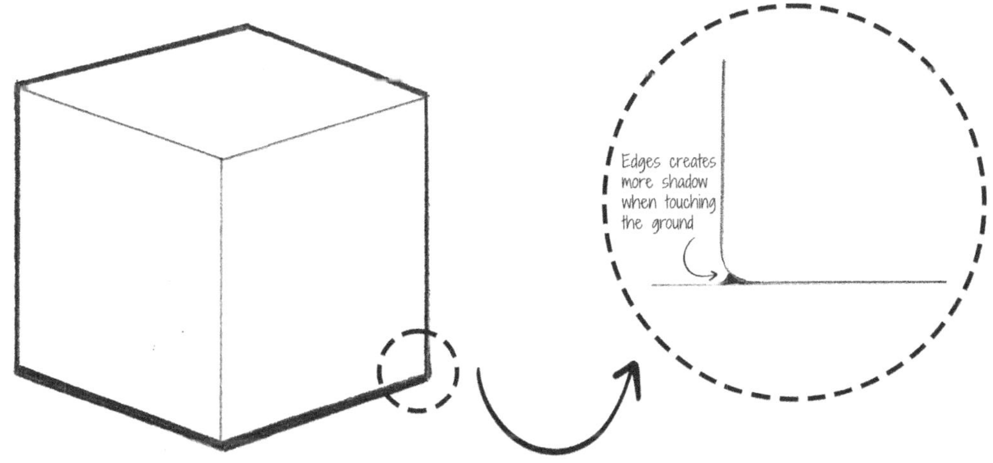

This makes the object pop off from the drawing surface more than it did when the lines were not given proper line weights. Additionally, there's no object that has a perfect, pointed corner edge. In that case, we make up those areas with extra thick lines. The reason for this is because those areas pick up more shadow and make the object appear more like it is sitting on the ground.

Now, let's move on from a basic cube to an object with more intricate details and identify where thick and thin lines ought to be placed.

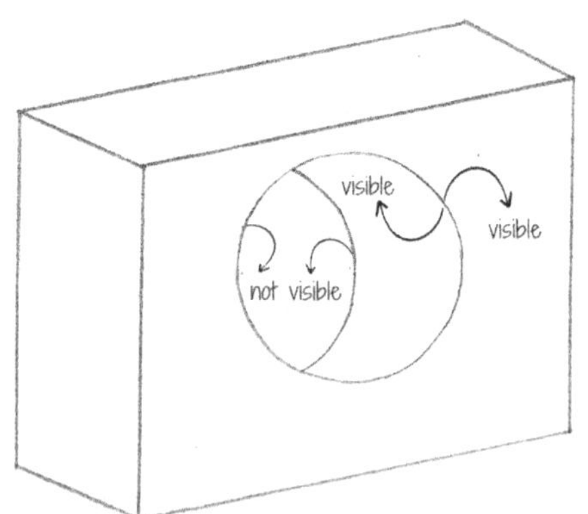

Let's say this is a rectangular piece of wood with a hole in the center. If you focus on the circle that makes up the hole, there's a part where you can see both surfaces, and there's a part where you can only see one side. How can you figure out what happens with the line?

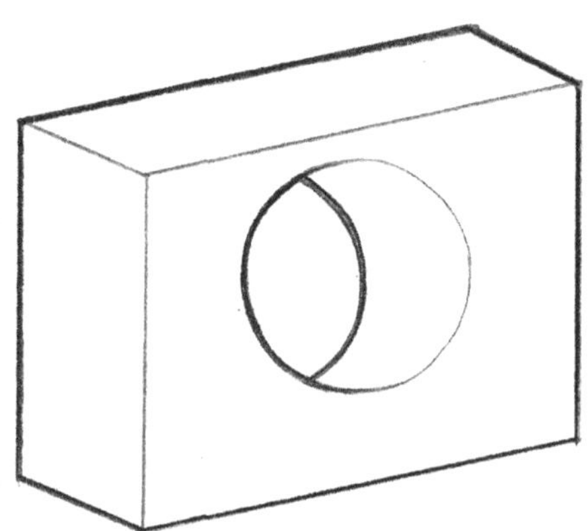

Well, it's very simple; there would be a transition from thick to thin line. The edge that only shows one side will still be a thick line, which will taper down to the edge where both surfaces are visible. Don't forget to thicken the outer edges of the object where one side is not visible.

Now that we all know where to put thick and thin lines on a certain object, we are going to place them in a scene. Let's begin with lighting.

In a scene with a light source, use thick or heavy lines for shadowed areas and thin lines in the area that is being hit by the light.

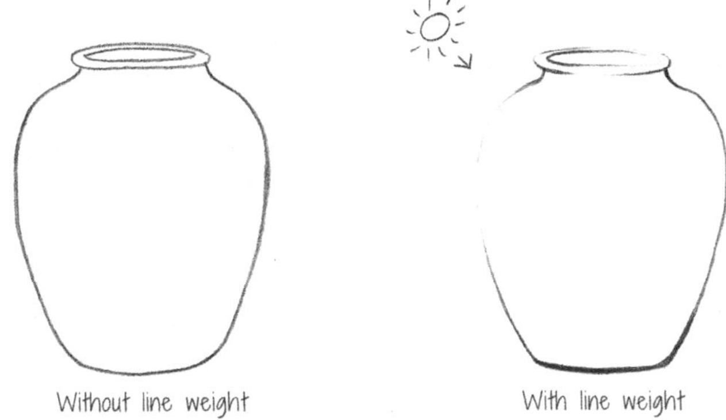

Let's take this jar for example: the lines become thicker in areas of shadow. There is a good mix of thin, medium, and heavy lines. Sometimes, in certain places where the light source is strong, lines can even be non-existent. This won't make the object appear unfinished, however. Instead, the human mind will see it as an illusion. This is what the power of lines can do!

Here's another example of a subject that has a light source:

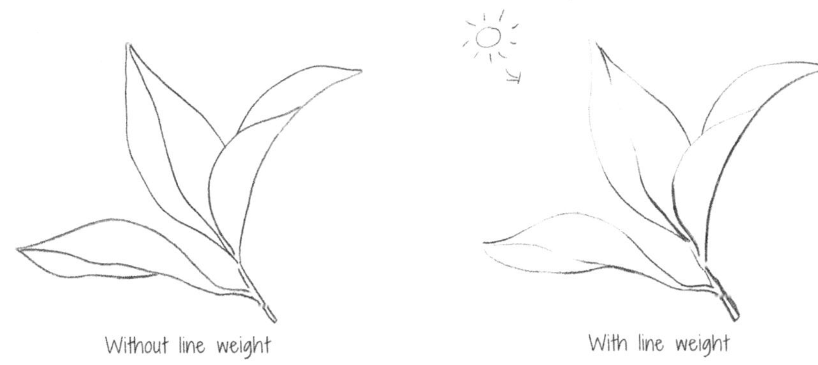

Notice how having line weights in the drawing on the right gives the leaves a more defined form.

The next scene we are going to tackle is distance. To emphasize distance in a drawing, remember that the closer the object, the thicker the line. Thin lines should be used for far-away objects.

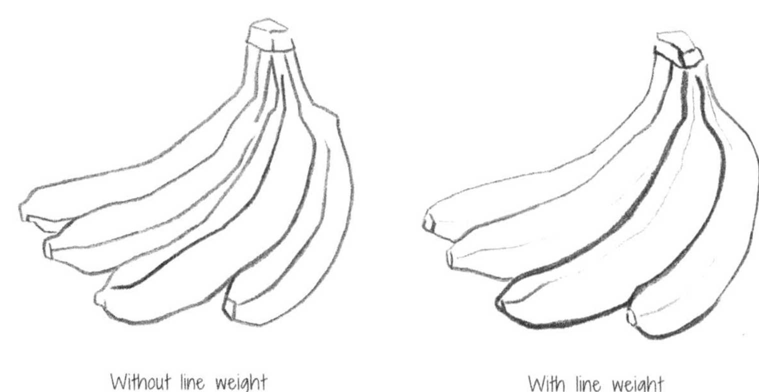

Without line weight

With line weight

By using this technique, you can manipulate the perception of the viewer. Let's take this banana as our subject. See how the closest finger in a bunch contains the thickest line and the others behind it have medium to thin lines.

Compare the drawing that has line weight to the drawing on the left. Notice how the left looks more cartoony. When your drawing has monotonous lines, it appears dull.

Here's another example of an object that emphasizes distance.

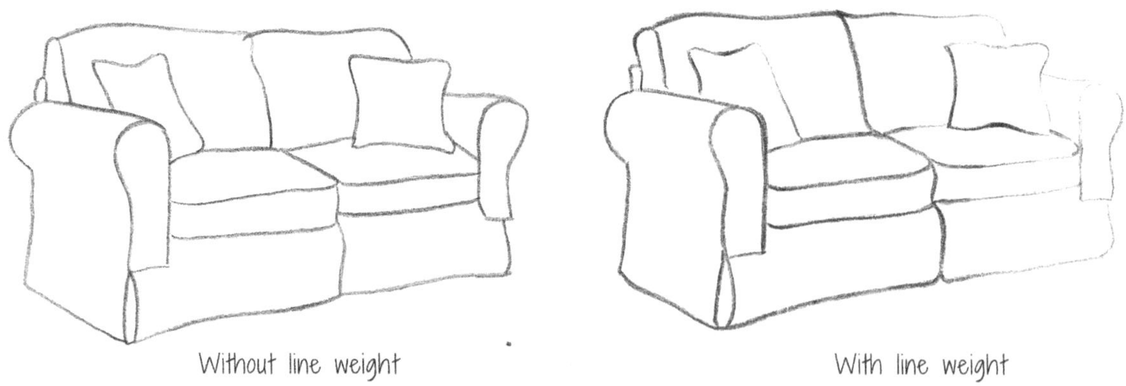

Without line weight

With line weight

Objects stretching far into distance become thinner and thinner. See how applying this technique makes the subject appear more realistic and gives it depth.

Now that you have an idea of how these techniques work on objects, let's try to combine everything you've learned.

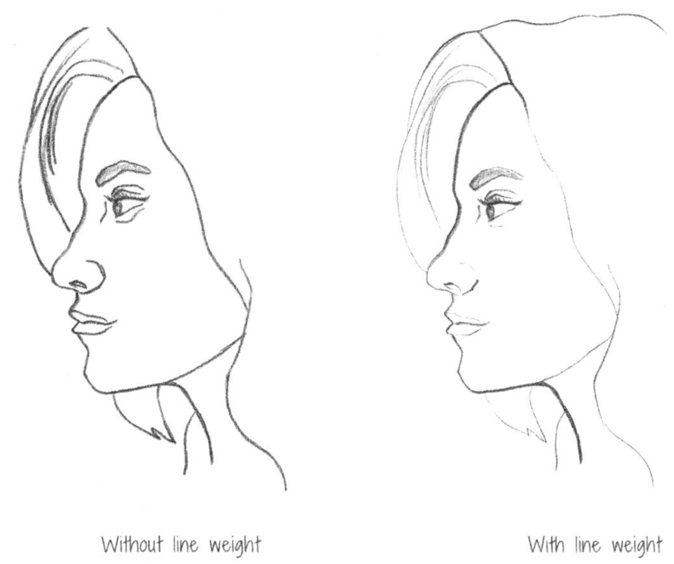

Here is a simple portrait. Try to observe the line weights in the drawing on the right. Notice how the thick lines are where the shadowed areas are. Assume that the light source is above her. Now, you might be wondering, in the case of distance, how come the hair facing our side has the same line weight with the hair on the other side?

In some cases, we can modify the way we want our viewers to see our drawings. With this one, I wanted to tell a story: I want the viewer's eyes to focus on the girl's facial features rather than on other things. Note that our eyes are drawn to thicker lines, and we, as artists, can use this to our advantage when we want to add drama to our artworks.

Holding a Pencil

There are different ways to hold the pencil when drawing, depending on what type of lines and strokes you are trying to achieve. By holding the pencil in different ways, we can create variety in our drawings right away. It's worth experimenting with different ways to hold a pencil. You could discover some that work better with your natural preferences. Here are some common hand grips:

BASIC/TRADITIONAL GRIP

The most common method for holding a pencil is what the title suggests. I believe this is how most of us hold a pencil, because this is the handwriting position, or general grip, used in writing and drawing. This grip allows for firm control over the pencil, and it utilizes the tip rather than the side of the pencil, which is ideal when creating fine details. Since this type of grip forces your hand to rest on the surface, you may use a spare sheet of paper to keep your drawing free from smudges and skin oils.

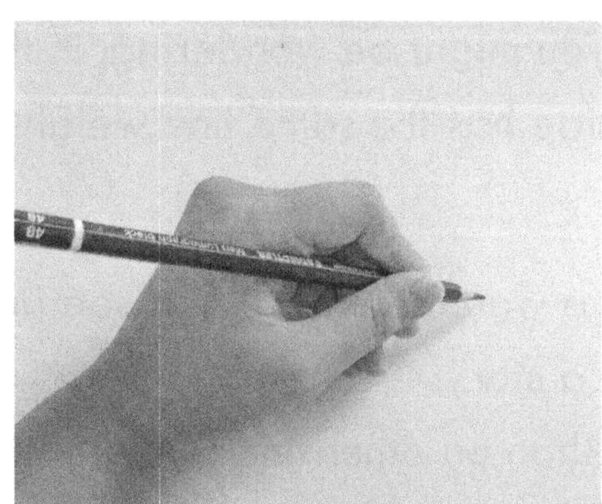

CREATE THIN, CONTROLLED LINES

EXTENDED GRIP

This grip is held in a similar manner to the handwriting position or the basic grip, except you hold the pencil out at a length. This grip is great for achieving light, delicate marks which can be wide, straight, and arched lines. Remember to keep your hold on the pencil relaxed when using this type of grip. Having a tight hold with this type of grip will restrict your movements and make your fingers tired at the same time. So, keep it loose, as the outcome of your sketch depends on this.

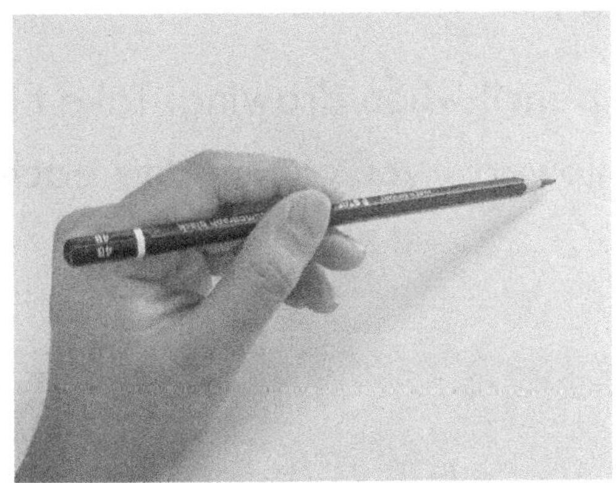

CREATE LONG, ARCING LINES

OVERHAND GRIP

When you need more pressure on your drawing, this is the perfect grip because it forces your pencil onto the surface. To use this grip, apply more pressure to the point of the pencil by moving your index finger closer to the tip. This grip allows you to use the side of the pencil, which is great for shading or thick lines that fill a large area in the drawing. Also, this is a useful pencil hold for vertical surfaces such as an easel.

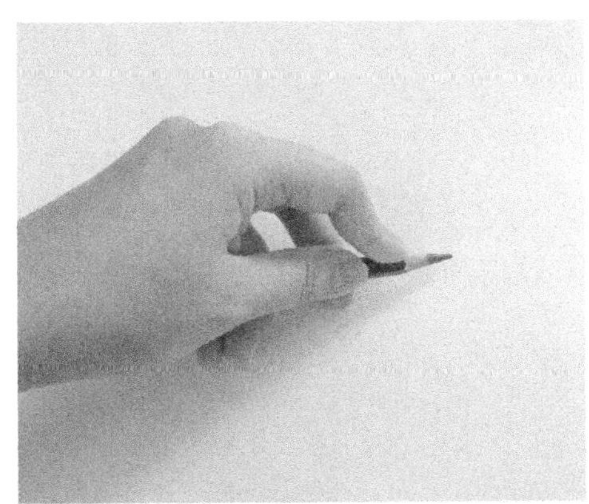

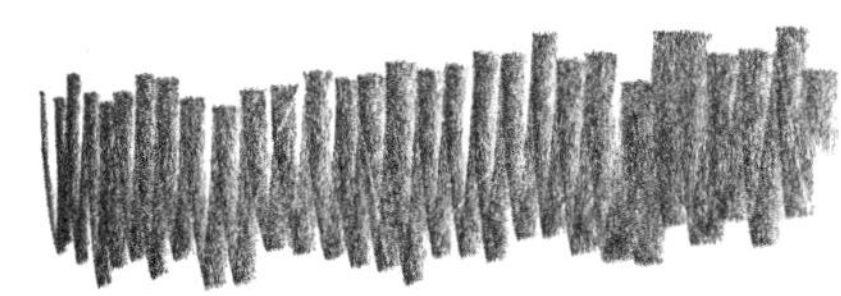

CREATE THICK, TIGHT LINES

UNDERHAND GRIP

This grip is a very loose and relaxed way of holding a pencil. It allows you to clearly see the marks as they are being drawn since your hand is out of the way. This is useful for casual and wide sketching, and great when using charcoal, especially when in the shading process.

These are the ways to properly hold a pencil when drawing. Take note that these techniques need not strictly be followed - you can modify each grip to suit your comfort.

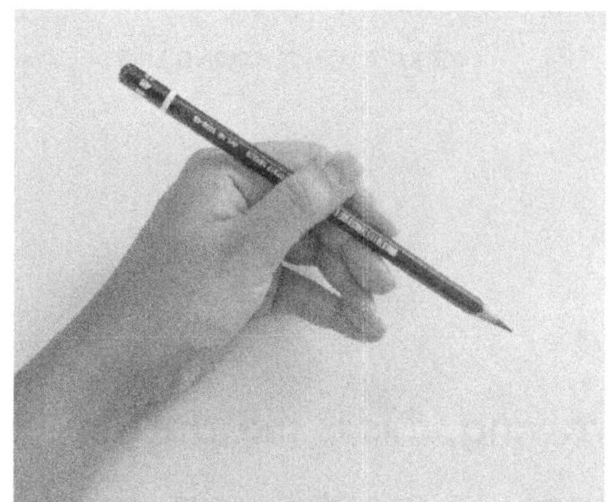

CREATE THICK, LOOSE LINES

Shading: Common Mistakes

BAD REFERENCE

One of the reasons your shading looks off, even when you have followed all the techniques you know, might be because you used a bad photo for your reference. Well, what makes a good reference photo? If you are not knowledgeable about photography, or are new to art, how can your eyes tell a good reference from a bad one? There are key points to look out for. Although this may seem easy in theory, for beginners, it still requires practice and patience. In the long run, your eyes will be able to tell immediately if a photo is good enough to be a reference for drawing.

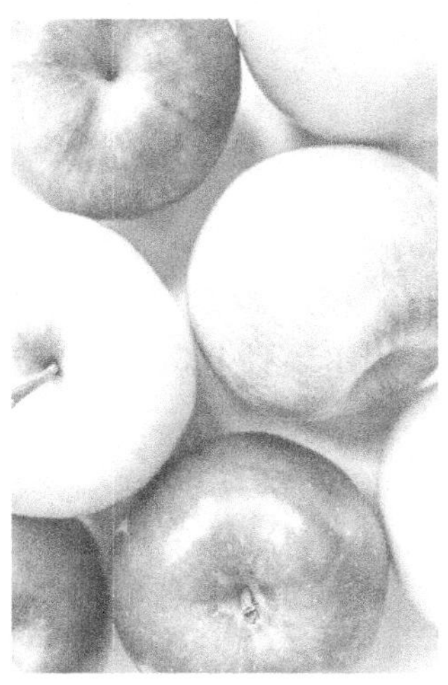

OVEREXPOSED

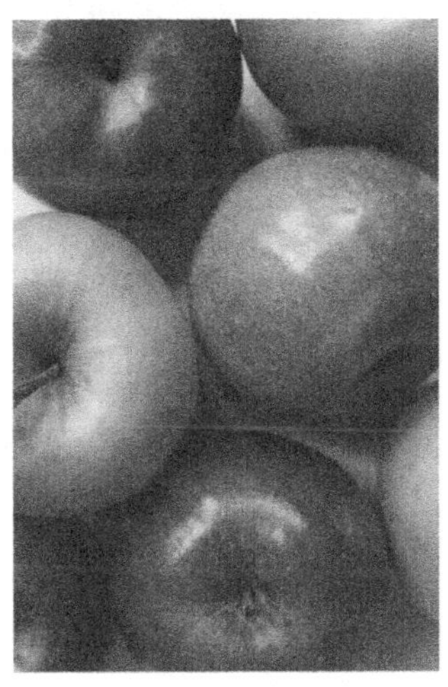

GOOD BALANCE

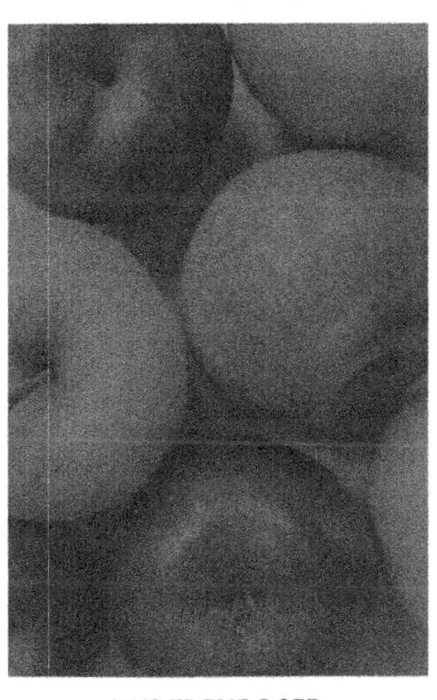

UNDEREXPOSED

Here are 3 key points to look out for:

Refer to the photo above to compare when it's over exposed, under exposed, and well-balanced.

Correct exposure – this means that the subject is neither too bright nor too dark and dull.

Shadows and highlights – Usually, when a photo has a good balance of shadows and highlights, it won't look overly contrasted.

High-definition – you'll know when an image is blurry right away. Now, why is a high-definition photo important for a reference? Because you'll be able to see all the details. The more details you draw, the more realistic your drawings will be.

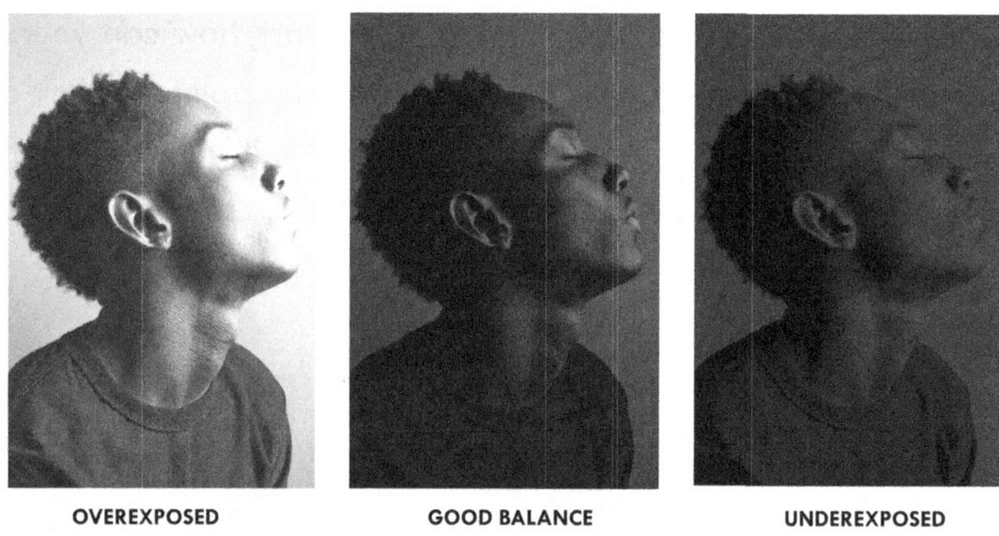

OVEREXPOSED GOOD BALANCE UNDEREXPOSED

Here's another example of a comparison photo. This time, a portrait. As you can see, it has all the 3 key points mentioned above; a good exposure, fine shadows and highlights, and it is in high definition.

Let's say our photograph has all the key points, except it's a tad over exposed. Should we not consider it anymore? Sure, you can keep working with it, and it's totally possible to create a fine drawing regardless, but it takes a good eye to be able to translate it into a balanced shading. It may take a while, but you'll get there.

ACCURACY

Every beginner's mistake when it comes to shading is getting excited about all the fancy, fun stuff without realizing that they're making a huge mistake in terms of proportion, and that some of their perspective is off. Having accuracy in all of your drawings is the important first step, because when you have the right proportions, structure, and form, everything else will follow.

You won't be able to create the right shading if you haven't achieved the simple forms and perspectives. In perspective, we also consider the light source. In our previous topic about light and shadows, you should have realized that both play a huge role when it comes to shading.

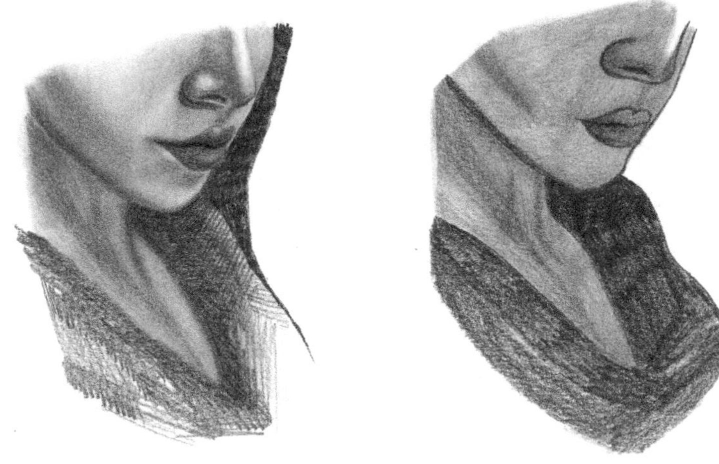

Here, you'll see two drawings. The one on the left has accurate proportions and careful shading, whilst the one on the right didn't bother much with accuracy and went right ahead with shading, making it look distorted and muddy. Regardless of whether you're drawing from life or using a reference, always study the subject first before digging in. Study and observe your subject carefully first, and then do your initial sketch and make sure it has the right proportions before finalizing it. When everything is perfect, you may shade the drawing. Shading and detailing are usually the last steps, so focusing on accuracy is a must. Always be patient.

OUTLINES

As beginners, we all start out drawing thick, dark outlines. This isn't a problem if you're drawing a cartoon, but to make your drawings look realistic, it's necessary to learn to regulate your outlines. Don't look at your subject as a 2D shape, but rather as a 3D plane. We mentioned this in our previous topic about line thickness and how lighting plays a huge role in it.

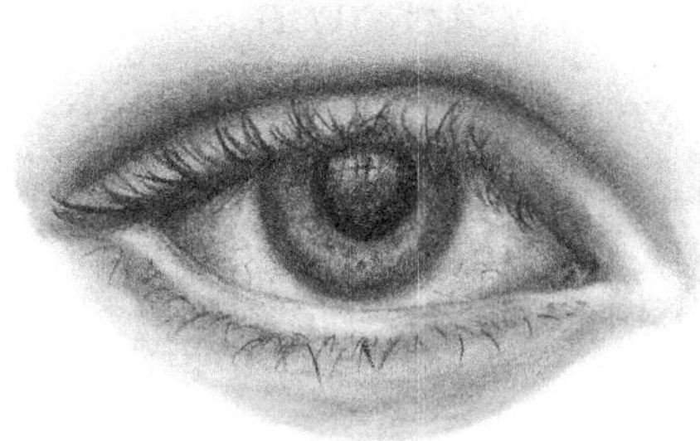

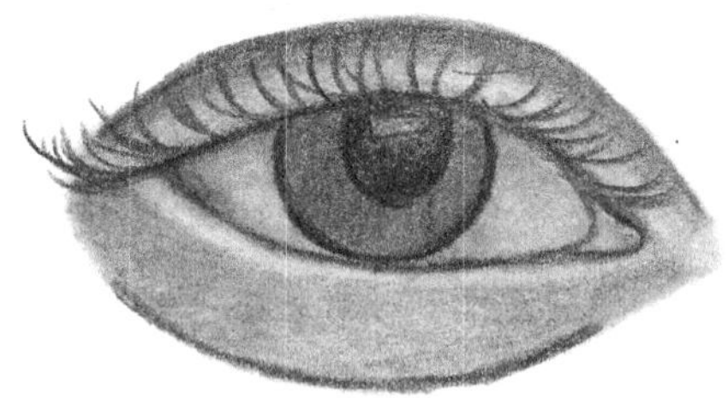

Sometimes, if you want to separate an area, you don't do so by adding outlines but rather by using proper shading. See the drawing above, for example. The crease of the eye is not a mere outline - it's composed of shadows, and proper shading has made it look folded and well-defined. The outline in the waterline of the eye is also drawn with subtlety to make it distinct from the eyeball. If you're using a reference photo, observe and study it. Eventually, you will notice the intricate details that make a drawing look more convincing.

SHADING DIRECTIONS

Whether you're using hatching, cross hatching, or another technique, it's still necessary to be cautious of the direction to make your shading look clean, decent, and more realistic. The shading might be messy because your hands get tired in one position, so you keep switching positions at the expense of clean, uniform shading. Shading can come in different directions, but it should be uniform, not just anywhere your hands go. Practice mindfulness when it comes to this, and you'll see how clean and artistic it will come out.

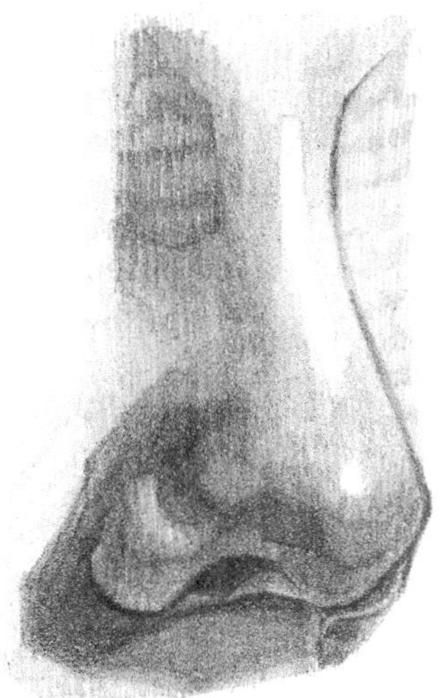
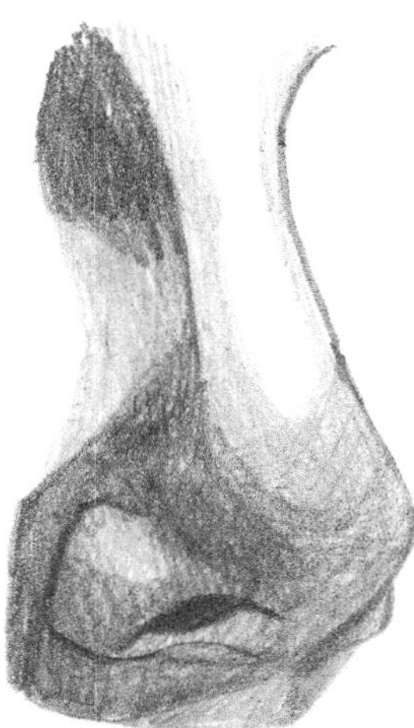

Above is an example of a nose that is shaded by hatching. Notice how a uniform direction made it look more convincing and neater.

ERASING AS HIGHLIGHTS

If you think that erasing is a method for providing highlights, your drawings may end up looking messy and muddy. Highlights are done by leaving the area unshaded or with a subtle shading. This depends on the amount of light that is hitting the subject.

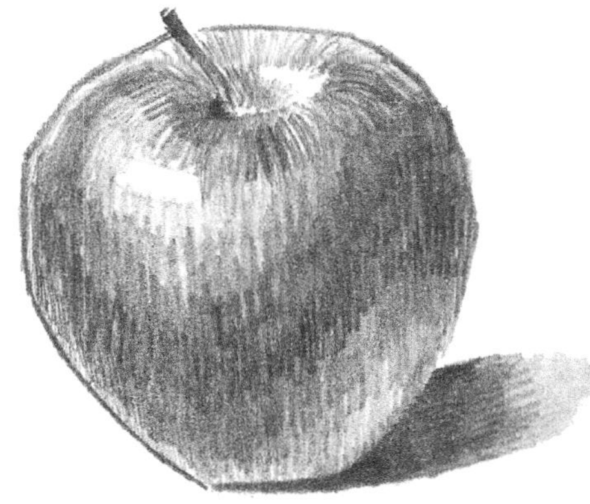
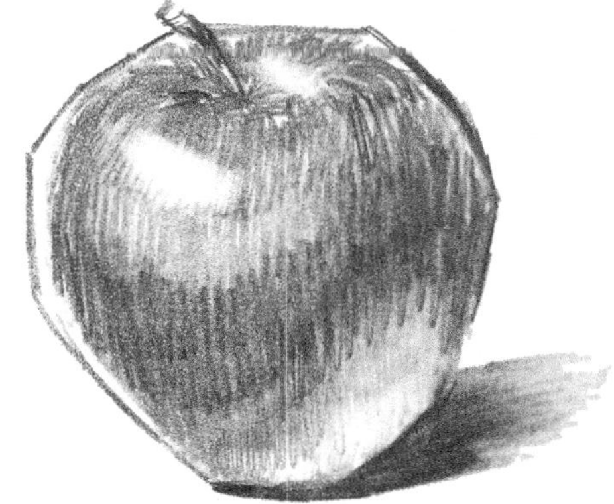

Whether you are using the blending technique or the simple hatches, the same principle applies. In the example of apples, the drawing on the left is an example of the correct way to produce highlights. On the right side is the outcome of when you use the erasing method for producing highlights in a drawing.

Remember to always be mindful of these common mistakes in shading. They may be the reason why your drawings are not looking as realistic and artistic as you'd like. Drawing takes a great deal of patience, but the outcome is worthwhile.

Blending

There are 6 common ways to blend charcoal and graphite pencils, making them a very versatile medium to work with. In this topic, we will tackle important variables such as pressure, the angle of the tool, and strokes. By the end, you will recognize how these aspects affect the results. Each blending method has its own advantages and disadvantages, making each of them unique in their own way.

The following techniques and principles are applicable both on graphite and charcoal.

LAYERING

This blending technique requires an understanding of the graphite/charcoal scale. It also takes some time and massive effort, as it requires repetition until the desired outcome is achieved. When using this method, always remember to do your layers slowly to achieve that smooth transition from light to dark tones.

Let's begin with the base layer. For the base, you may use a mid to high H pencil. In this example, I used 5H. Fill the whole sketch with 5H using a light pressure. As for the strokes, you may do hatching or, for a smoother effect, use circling without gaps all throughout the layers.

Then, layer a mid-range pencil on top. That's either an H, F, HB, or B pencil. This time, don't shade the whole thing. Instead, be mindful of the values. Usually, these pencils are for light midtones. Use light to medium pressure.

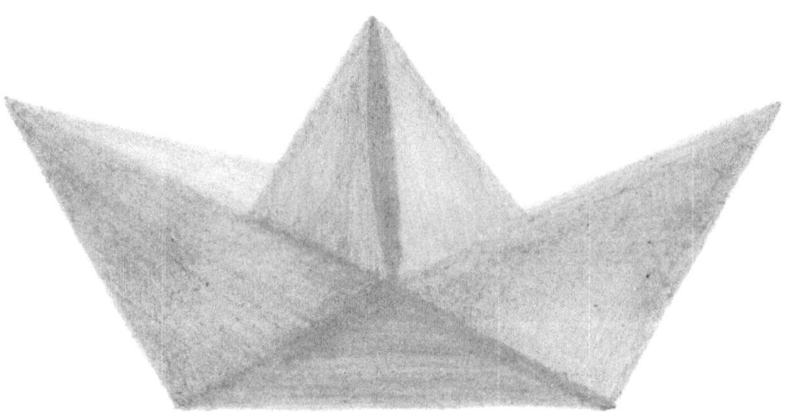

The next layer would be a bit darker than the previous one. You would therefore use a soft, B pencil of your choice. For this drawing sample, I used a 2B. For this tone, shade the dark midtones and play with light, using medium pressure on the pencil.

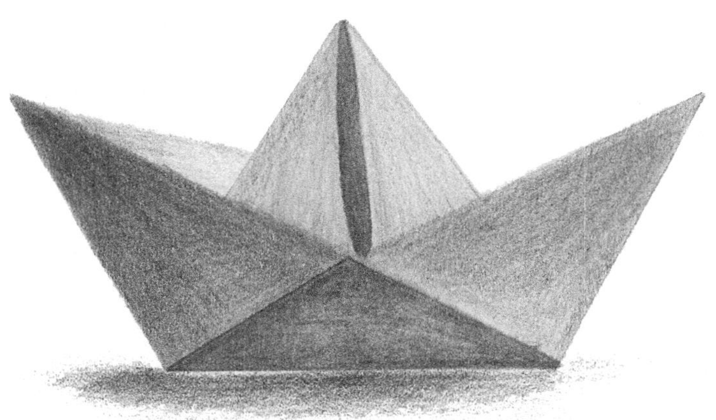

For the last layer and the darkest area, which are the shadows, use 4B and apply medium to heavy pressure.

This technique is time consuming, but when done right, it produces a great outcome. It also takes patience to achieve those smooth gradients without the support of an additional tool. This method is the main base for the techniques that require a tool. We will tackle that next.

BURNISHING

Burnishing is a kind of blending method that is different from simply layering the pencil grades. This method also uses a firm, heavy pressure, unlike in layering. The primary goal of this method is to hide the texture or tooth of the paper, thus the heavy pressure. The outcome may depend on the paper you use, so do some experimenting with this technique, and you may desire this look on some of your drawings.

In this technique, you can skip the harder pencils and just jump directly to a mid-grade pencil. For this sample, we used an HB grade pencil as the base and applied layering with light to medium pressure.

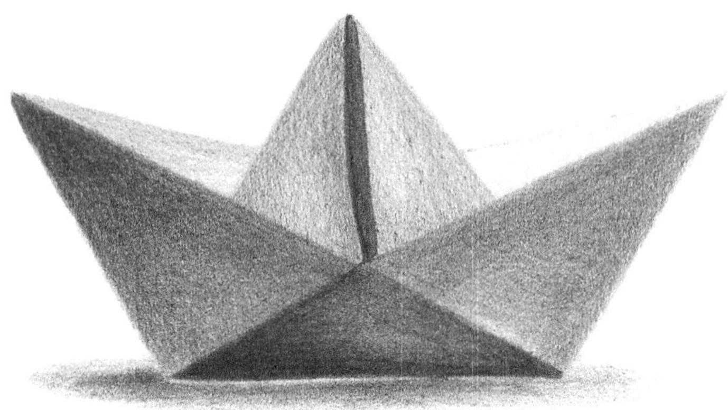

For the last application, you may use a soft pencil, for instance, a 4B, and get a similar shade when you use an 8B. Apply heavy pressure on the dark parts to push or "burnish" the initial layer of graphite deeper into the tooth of the paper. The strokes may be done in one-direction hatching or circling.

PAPER STUMPS

Be it a blending stump or tortillon, they can be used in a similar way in blending. However, they may lead to different results, depending on what you wish to achieve. This technique is great for facial features in portraiture.

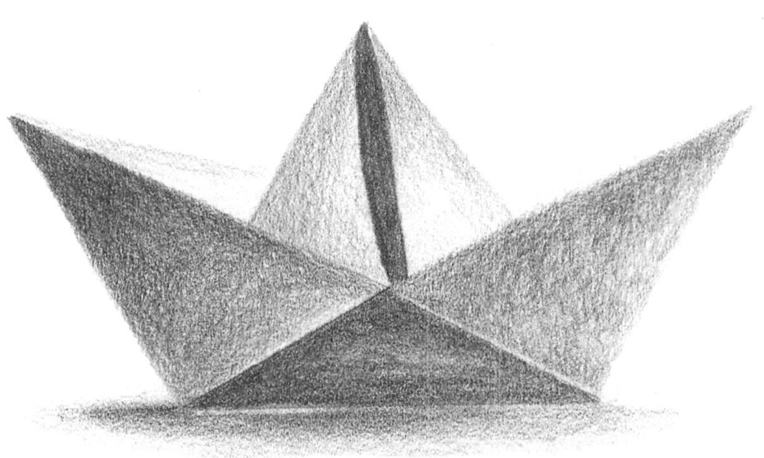

Begin by shading with a soft grade. We used a 4B for this sample all throughout, although you may add darker grades later to achieve your desired outcome. The strokes can be hatching or circling with light to medium pressure. As for the lightest areas, you may skip shading them and instead use the residual graphite left in the paper stump to fill in the area. Just make sure that, when you do this, you apply light, repeated pressure to avoid uneven shading.

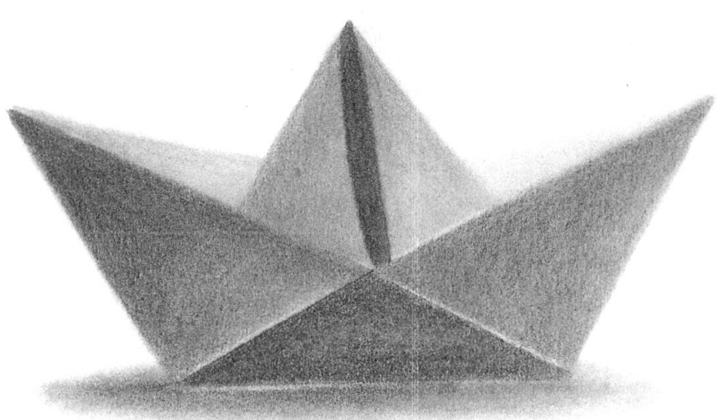

To blend, if you're using a blending stump, use the tip for corners or small details, and use the sides at an angle for broad areas. For tortillon, make sure that your angle is consistent to avoid graphite or charcoal bumps. Blend in a circular motion with light pressure on the highlighted areas and midtones, and heavy pressure on the shadowed or darker areas. Take caution, however, as excessive pressure may damage the texture of the paper, which may be difficult to fix.

Q-TIPS

Another way to blend is using q-tips or cotton balls for broad areas. This is helpful when blending details in facial features and skin to achieve a smooth effect. Q-tips are also very cost effective and cheap, so you can replace them right away and use a new, clean one whenever you need to.

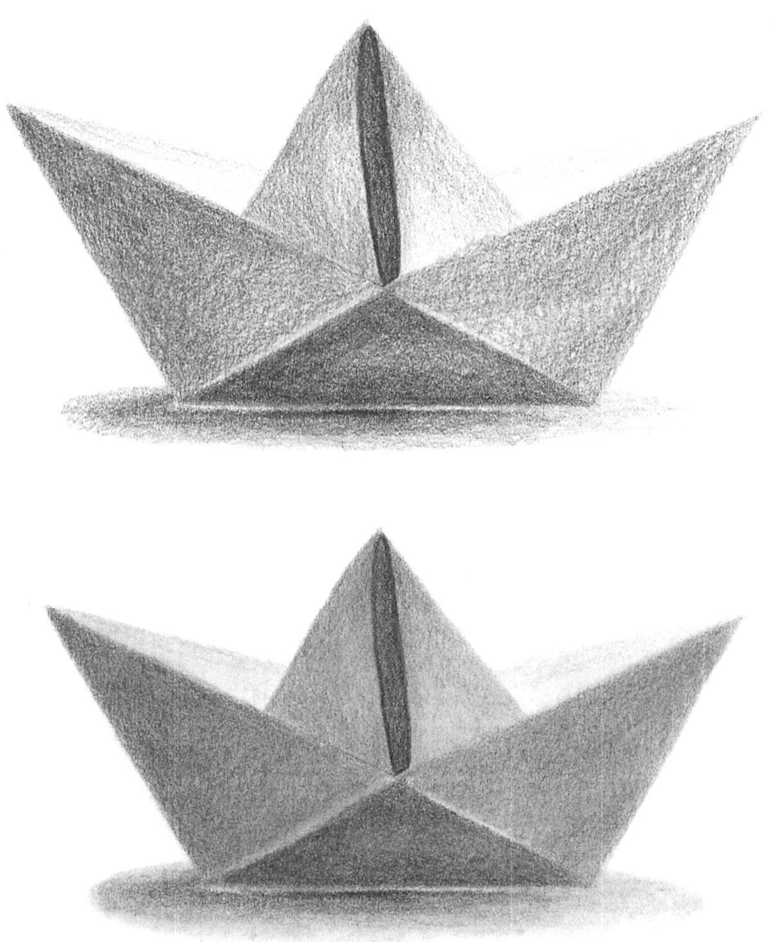

The first step will always be shading and layering. Once you're satisfied with the shading, proceed with blending. For this tool, blend in circular or single, sweeping motions with light to medium pressure. Heavy pressure may also be used on darker areas. Because q-tips are smooth, they are unlikely to damage the texture of the paper. Additionally, they still leave a smooth area behind, which is almost, but not 100%, similar to the outcome when using a blending stump.

BRUSHES

Brushes for blending can be paint brushes or makeup brushes. Normally, puffy brushes are in the makeup category while firm and flat brushes are available in art shops. The brush technique is great for blending the skin and hair in a portrait.

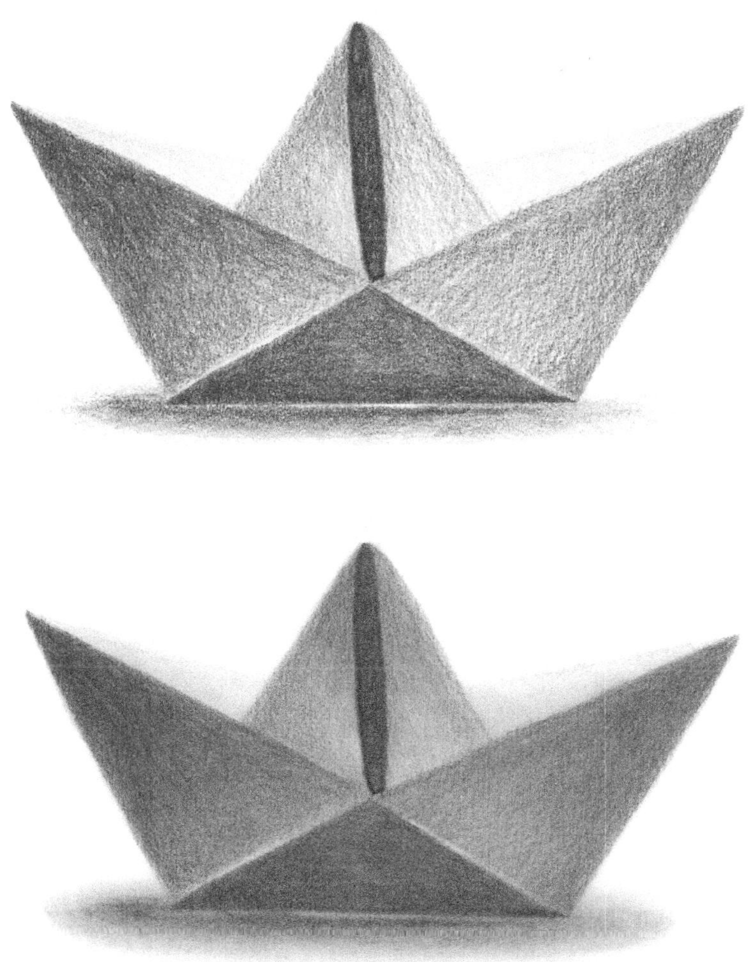

After shading and layering, pick up the brush of your choice to blend. Blending with a brush is usually done in a circular motion with light pressure. This should be done repeatedly. Use the flat brush for sharp ends or corners and a puffy brush for broad areas. As you can see, the result is very smooth, which is why this technique is perfect for blending the skin in a portrait. However, keep in mind that the smoothness may vary depending on the paper you use.

TISSUE

When using tissue for blending, make sure it's the smooth kind and not the textured kind. Also, make sure it's plain, dry, and not infused with any liquid or moisturizer.

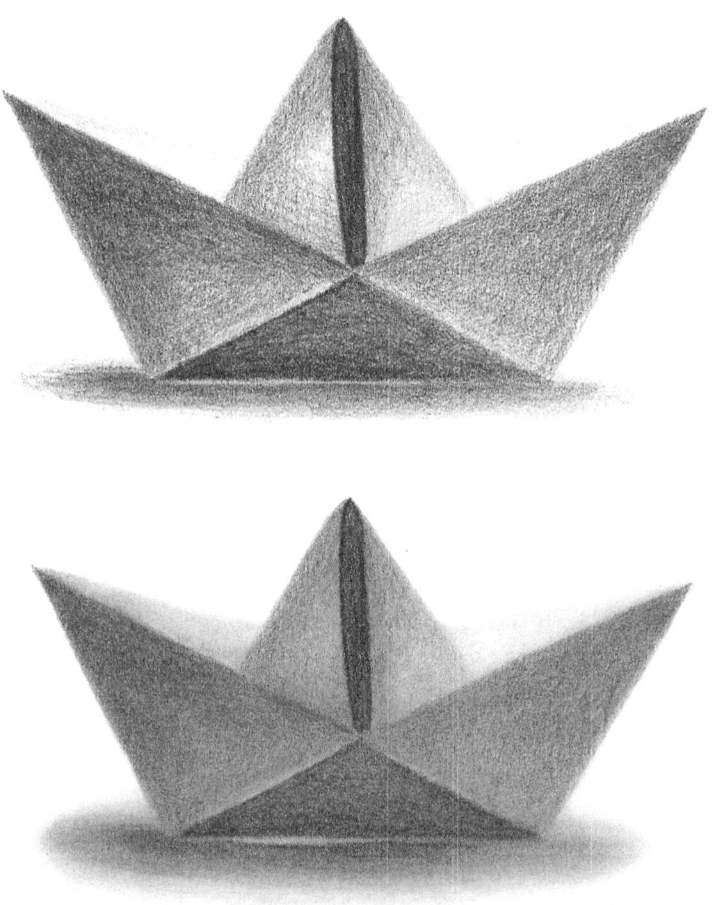

When using this tool for blending, wrap it around your finger and blend in circular motions with light to medium pressure. Make sure the pressure you apply is constant on the whole area to avoid any uneven parts. This makes a great blender for skin in portraits. If you need to reach the narrow areas, you may fold or twist the tissue to keep a crisp edge. You may also need to rework the shading because the tissue may remove a bit of graphite or charcoal from the paper. But, if done with patience, you may achieve a smooth outcome using a cost-effective material.

Here's how it looks when charcoal is used. The paper stump and q-tips left it appearing darker, while the brushes and tissue made it appear lighter. This is because those tools pick up the charcoal more, which is also the reason they're great for skin and other areas that need a smoother blend. The paper stump and q-tips, on the other hand, are great for details and darker areas.

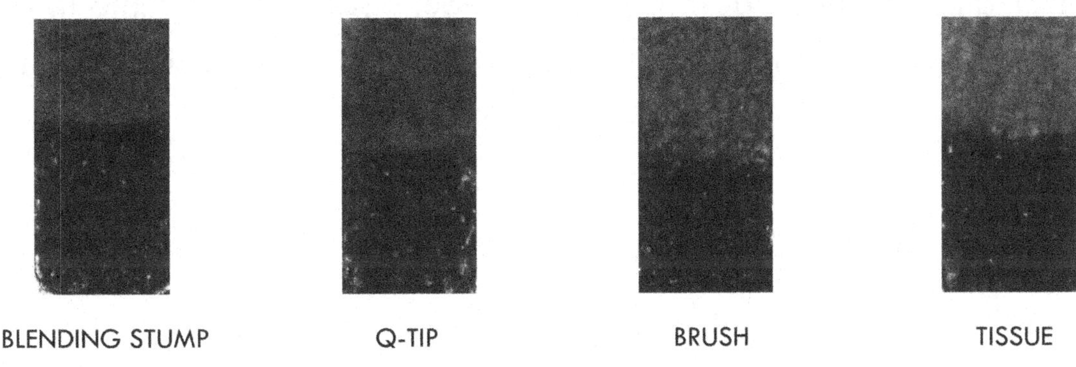

Drawing Tips and Tricks

Drawing is a skill. If you're learning to draw an apple today, tomorrow you'll be able to draw the Monalisa. Just kidding, it doesn't work like that. It takes time, consistency, discipline, and patience, just like every skill we learn. You can draw better and be skilled at it if you pour your heart and soul into it. Here are some tips and tricks for beginners that will help you elevate your skill in drawing.

GET INTO THE HABIT OF DRAWING REGULARLY

By regularly, I mean don't be too hard on yourself. Your drawings don't always have to be grand. Instead of committing to large chunks, try doing little rough sketches or doodles each day. This doesn't need planning - sketch anything your mind can think of at the moment or do a plein air study. Just do anything to get those creative juices flowing. Also, it doesn't have to take much time; it can be a 5 or 10-minute sketch. Just dedicate a small amount of time to drawing daily. Practice daily to develop your skills.

START WITH STRAIGHT LINES

When drawing, make sure everything is correct and that you're satisfied before finalizing it with darker, bold lines. There's no harm in taking time doing the light sketch. What matters most is that drawing comes out clean and accurate. If you're just doodling random sketches, it doesn't matter if you don't erase the light lines as your guide. A messy, imperfect sketchbook is okay. It's called "sketch" for a reason!

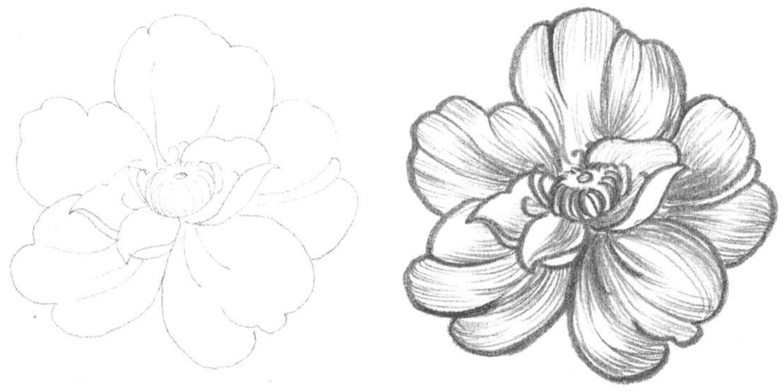

VARIETY

When practicing, don't limit yourself to just one subject. Get outside your comfort zone and try to draw the vast variety of possible subjects in the world, like animals, house objects, scenery, buildings, and much more! This is also a great way to help you out of an art block!

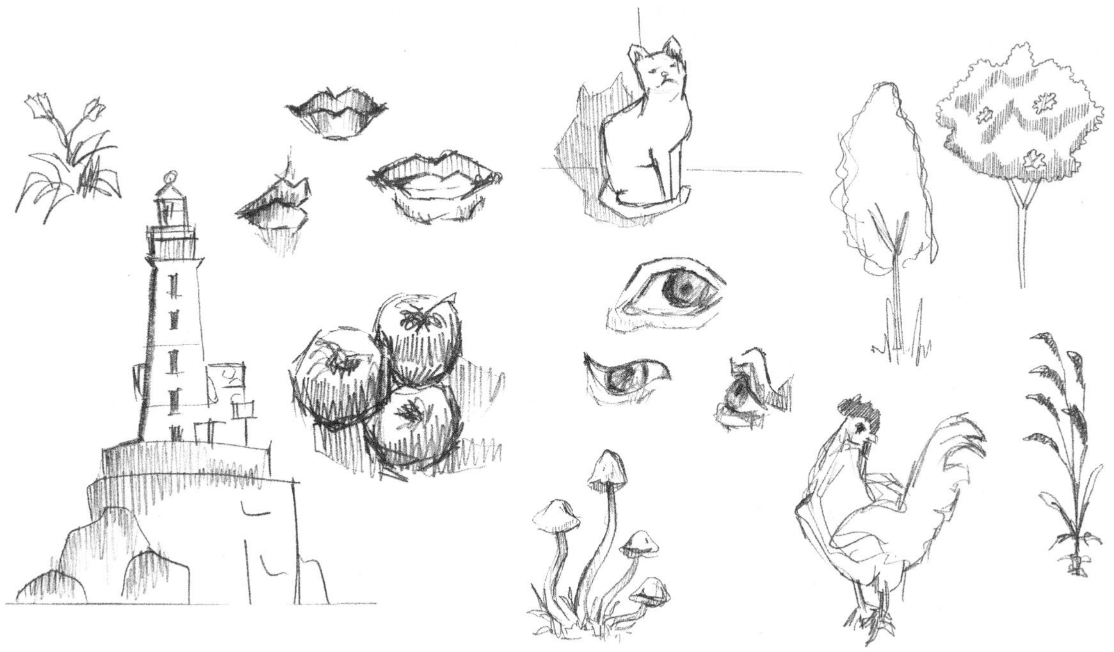

DRAW UPSIDE DOWN

This exercise may seem odd but, believe me, it works and can help you improve! The primary goal of this exercise is to make you focus on what you see because, most of the time, people tend to draw what they know. Drawing upside down enhances how you recognize shapes and lines in a picture rather than simply seeing the whole thing.

This exercise is mostly helpful in portraiture. We tend to pick up the main features of a face and draw them in a snap. This is because our brain thrives on understanding its surroundings quickly, and this ability is much stronger when we see faces. When we do this, we tend to miss the simple, yet important, details in every face that we draw. This exercise will help you to become aware of the distinct lines and shapes of the subject as you draw. So, next time you try drawing regularly, you'll know right away where to situate your focus.

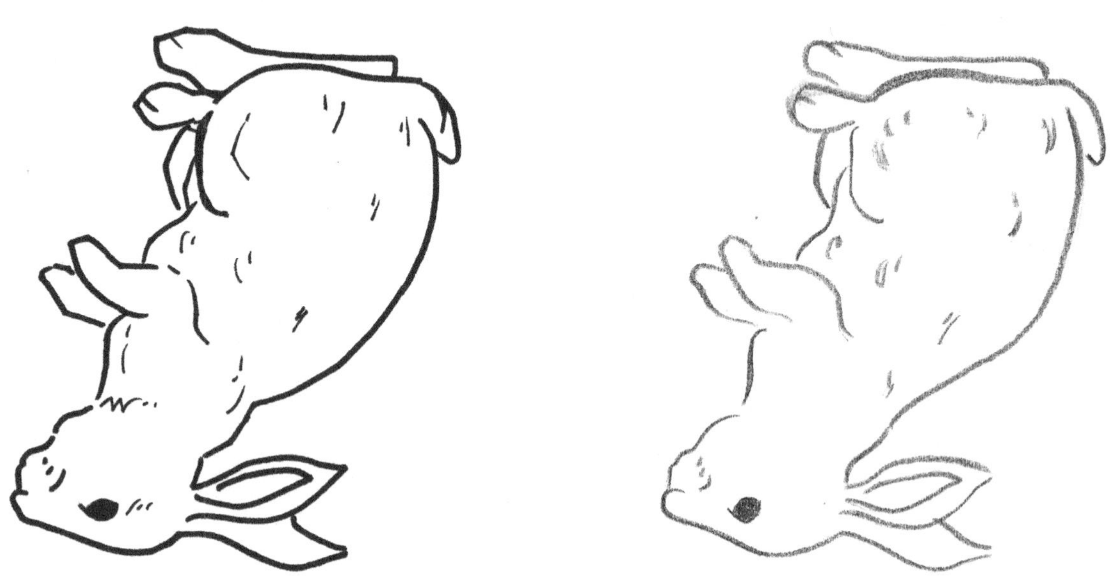

DEVELOP HAND-EYE COORDINATION

This is not just applicable in sports! Whether you're drawing from life or from a photograph reference, this skill is essential for progress to occur, especially when you're trying to achieve a certain level of realism. In portraiture, having references allows us to develop our observational skills and our hand-eye coordination. This is an important skill to practice because it's impossible for the human brain to hold on to all the visual information we see in front of us.

MASTER THE ART OF OBSERVATION

Drawing is about seeing. Unless you are drawing from imagination, you don't just dig into your sketchbooks, right? Before you draw anything, study your reference carefully. By study, I mean observe the basic shapes you see, the angle, the perspective, the scale, the values, the shadows and highlights, and those tiny details that are usually not immediately noticeable to our vision. When you have a portrait as a reference, try to notice all the tiny details that will make your drawing look more realistic. Also, by observing, you are planning in your head the steps you'll take when you start to sketch.

I suggest that the amount of time you should spend looking at your subjects should be half the time it takes to complete the drawing. In short, don't fret when it takes longer for you to observe and completely absorb your subject, as it will be easier to draw correctly after that.

Practice observing anything, whether you're at the park or at the mall. Observe the trees, the sky, the benches, the people, their movements, the flow of the water in the river, or basically anything in your surroundings. Try to notice as many details as you can. This can be a great exercise for mastering the art of observation.

DON'T BE DISCOURAGED

Learning how to draw won't happen overnight. You'll feel discouragement at times and that's for sure, but this doesn't mean it's the end for you. Remember, everyone was once a beginner. Practice consistently, yes, but rest if you must. Learning to draw is a journey. There's no need to be in a hurry, as you'll eventually get there. Even those artists you admire now are still hungry for progress because it's a never-ending process of learning. Don't be afraid of making mistakes because, surely, you'll always learn from these mistakes and improve with your next artwork. Try this challenge: compare your drawings from 6 months or 1 year ago, when you started, to the art you're creating now. You'll definitely see some progress and it will make you feel motivated to keep improving.

Eye

The eye is the most expressive feature on the face, so it's important to draw and shade it correctly. Let's begin.

Step 1: Draw the guideline.

Using an HB pencil, draw, lightly, a vertical and horizontal line that will form a cross. This will be your guide on where to draw a circle. Next, draw a big circle in the center and two smaller ones inside it. This will resemble an eyeball.

Step 2: Sketch the outline

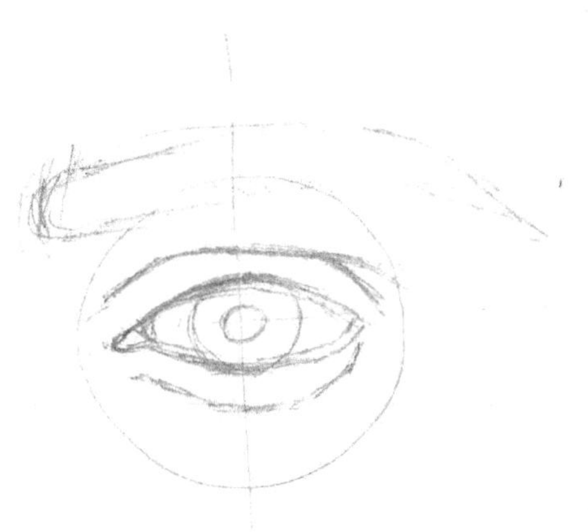

Now, draw the outline or contours of the eye, still using an HB pencil and without pressing too hard. Do not forget the important elements of the eye that are often neglected, such as the waterline under the eye and the inner corner elements. At this stage, you may also sketch the eyebrow.

Step 3: Shade the pupil

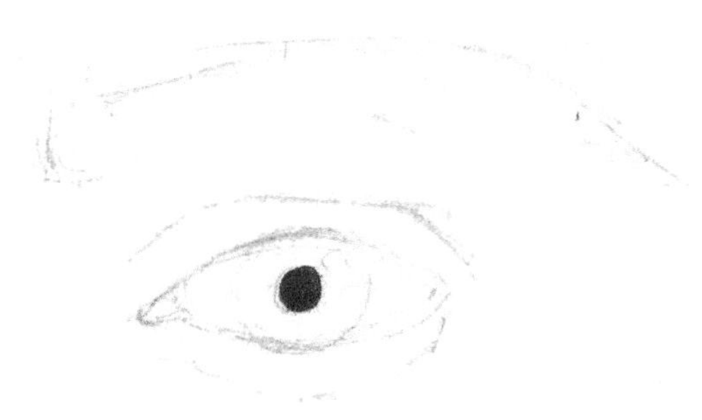

When your outlines are perfect in terms of proportions, you may now erase the guidelines. Make sure to erase them carefully so you don't erase the main outline you did of the eye and eyebrow. Next, use a kneaded eraser to erase the outline slightly. Make sure it is very light but still visible. Now, you can start shading the pupil using a 6B or the darkest grade of your choice. Avoid pressing so hard that it will be difficult to erase if you make a mistake. Also, keep the highlights clean.

Step 4: Darken the outline

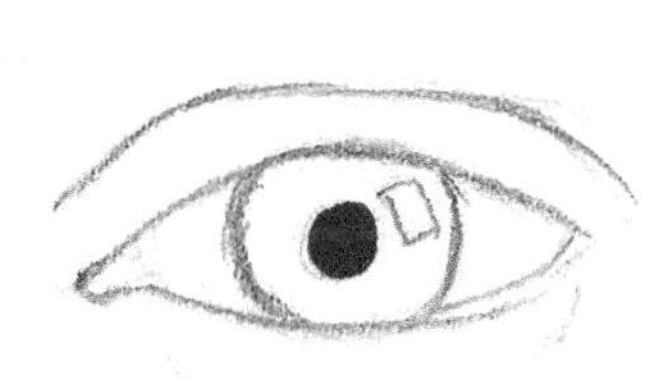

The next step is to darken the outline using a 4B but, again, don't press too hard. Darken the outline of the eye except for the eye wrinkle. Then, draw a rectangular shape inside the iris. This will serve as the light reflection. This may differ from every eye or the style of your choice, but for this guide, let's stick with the basics.

Step 5: Shade the iris

Using a 2B pencil, shade or hatch the iris lightly.

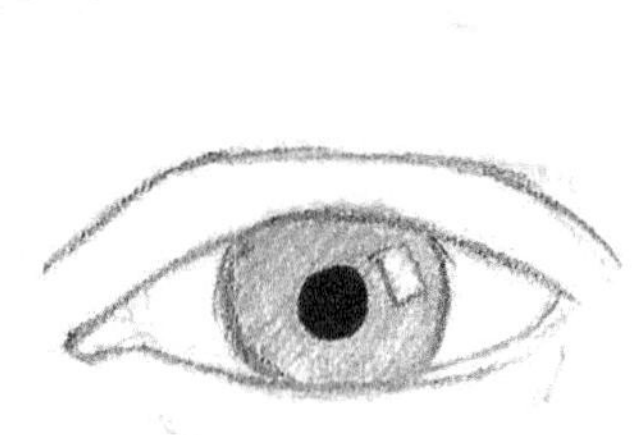

Step 6: Draw spokes

Now, using a 4B pencil, draw spokes outward from the pupil. This will make the eye drawing more visually appealing. Make sure not to fill everything with spokes - leave some areas untouched, as they will be filled in later. Maintain the cleanliness of the light reflection.

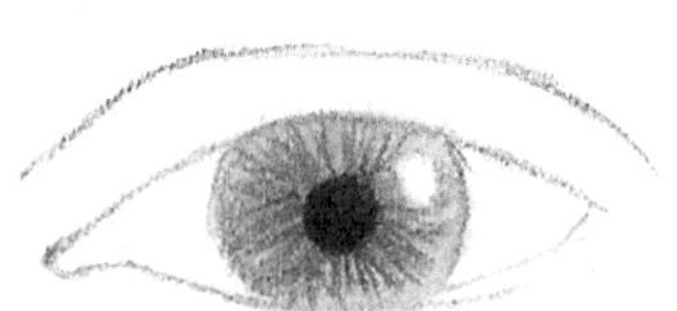

Step 7: Blend outline of the iris

The next step is to blend the iris. Using a blending stump, blend in a circular motion from the pupil outwards while maintaining the cleanliness of the light reflection. Also, using a 4B, draw outlines on the outer part of the pupil.

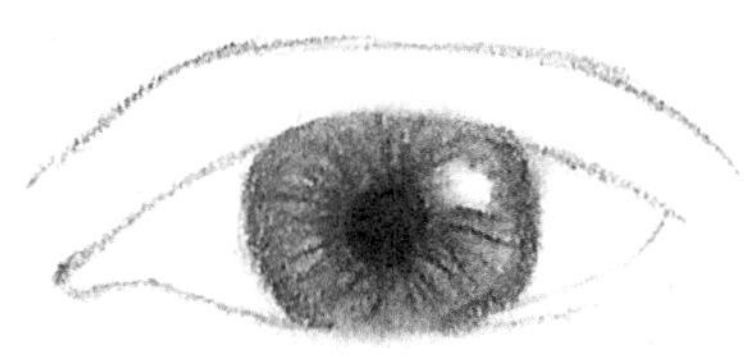

Step 8: Shade the sclera

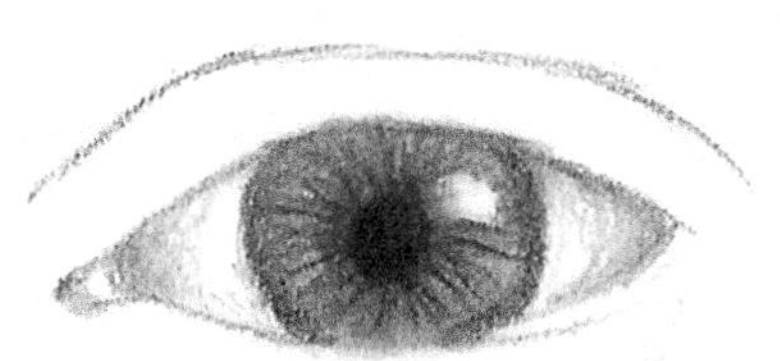

Using a 4B, shade the sclera and the inner corner element. Make sure to shade lightly because we will blend this in later. When blending the sclera, the part near the iris should be lighter while the outer area is darker. For the inner corner element, usually it is divided into halves. As you can see in the drawing, the left part is shaded and the other half on the right is left blank. This will create an illusion that it is wet.

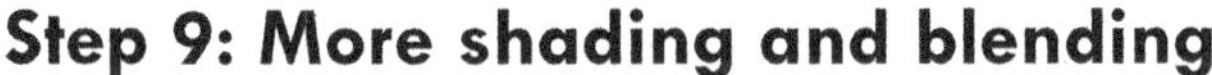

Step 9: More shading and blending

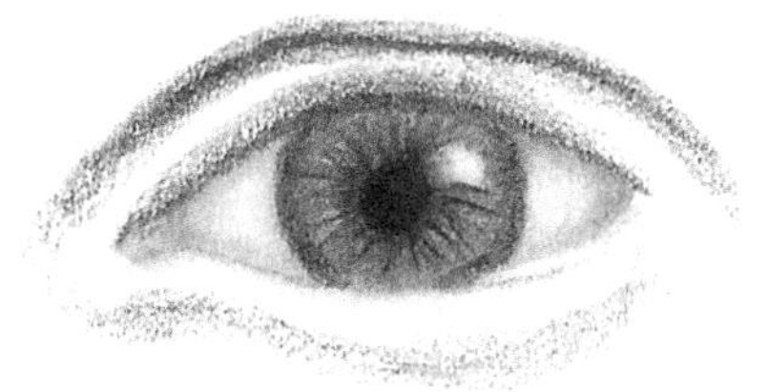

Using a blending stump, blend the sclera. Start from the outer area, going inwards to the pupil. Next, using a 4B, lightly shade the area in the crease, upper eyelid, outer corner of the eye, and the under-eye wrinkle. Shade everywhere except for the under eyelid.

Step 10: Greater shadings

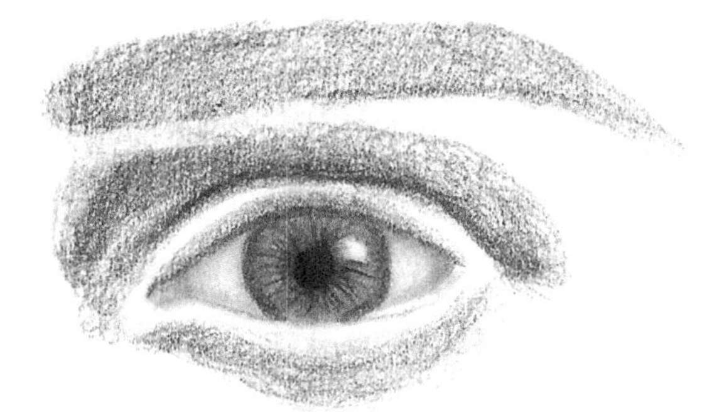

Do not blend yet. Instead, using 4B, do more shading on the elements you've shaded before using a circular motion, this time, on a greater area outward from the first shading. At this stage, be aware of the values. You may press the 4B harder or lighter depending on said values. Also, start lightly shading the eyebrow using 4B as well.

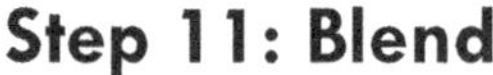

Step 11: Blend

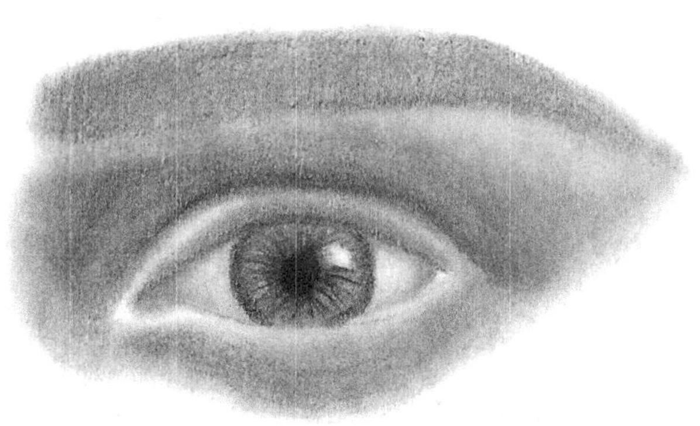

Now, blend everything using a blending stump. When you blend, make sure you go from lighter to darker areas and not vice versa. Don't worry if the highlights become a bit darker, as this can be fixed later.

Step 12: Emphasize highlights

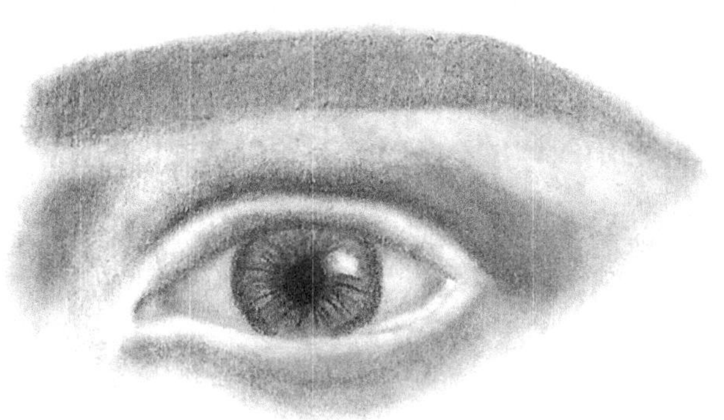

Using a kneaded eraser, tap lightly on the highlighted parts of the eye to emphasize them. Don't overdo this because you might erase the shadows, which are difficult to fix.

Step 13: Outlines

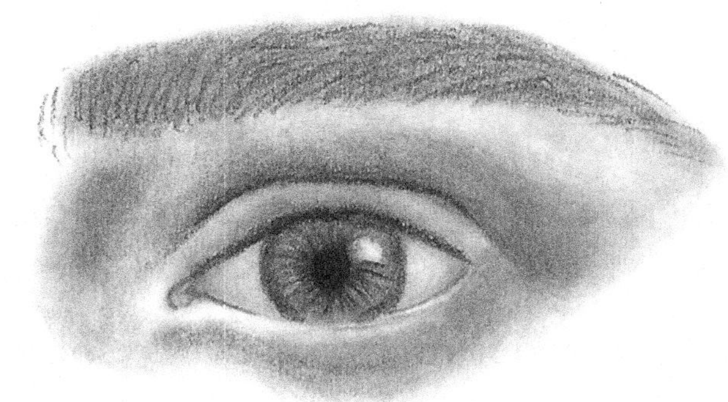

Using a 4B pencil, draw outlines once again on the crease, inner corner element, and upper eyelid. Use 2B for the under eyelid. Make sure that the waterline is not shaded to create an illusion that this is the wet part of the eye. Using a 4B, draw strokes on the eyebrow. Follow the direction of the shape that you drew.

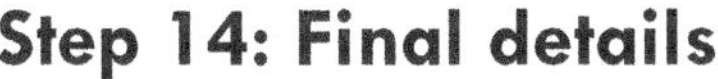

Step 14: Final details

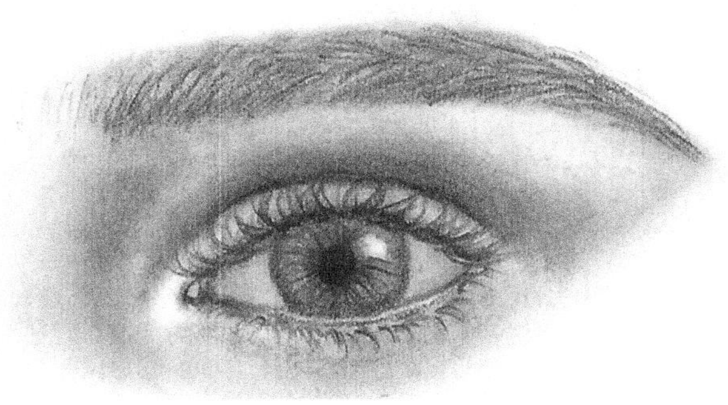

For the last step, using a kneaded eraser, lightly dab on the part where the highlights must be emphasized. Also, using the kneaded eraser, erase using strokes on the eyebrow to create an illusion of hairs. To complete the eye, draw the eyelashes using a 6B that is sharp or pointy. Eyelashes are always the last part in drawing the eye because they are drawn using a darker grade, and once drawn, they cannot be fixed.

Nose

The nose is a rather challenging feature because it sticks out of the face and, therefore, its appearance varies depending on the viewpoint of the observer. Also, if not the eye, the nose is the 2nd most difficult feature to perfect in drawing portraits since it is composed mainly of shading and blending. For the sake of realism, the outlines must be kept to a minimum. Alright, let's begin.

Step 1: Start with guidelines

Using an HB pencil, start by drawing a circle, this will be the determiner of how pointy the nose you're going to draw will be. The smaller the circle, the pointier and longer the resulting nose. For this, let's do a typical nose. Next, draw two vertical lines on ¼ of both sides of the circle. And a horizontal line below ¼ of the circle. Then draw two diagonal lines that connect the vertical and horizontal ones. This depends on how wide or slim you want to make the nose.

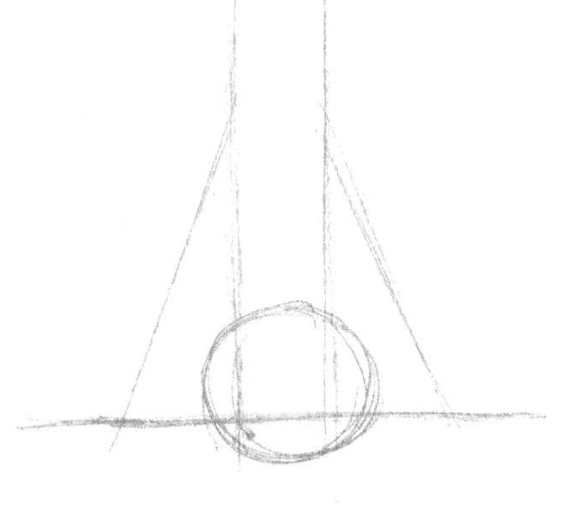

Step 2: Outline

Now, using a 4B, follow the shape you drew to make the outline for the nostrils and the tip of the nose. Remember, these will be the only outlines for the nose. The rest of the shape is made up through shading.

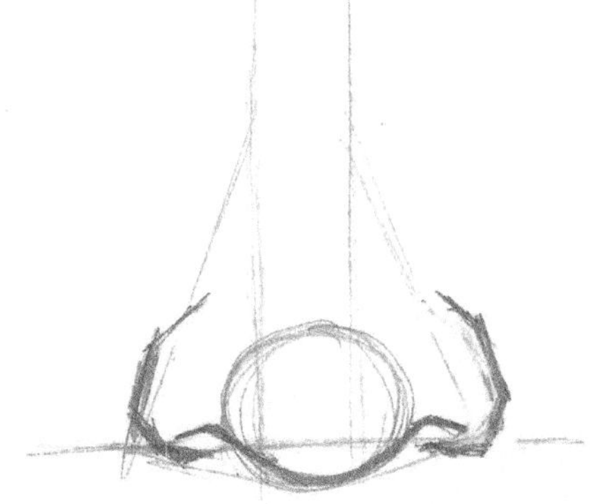

Step 3: Clean and prepare

Now that you have the shape of the nose, you may erase the guidelines, very lightly if you still want a guide, or completely if you don't. Clean and finalize the outline of the nostrils and tip.

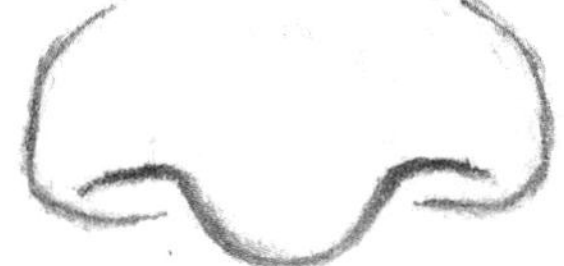

Step 4: Shading

Now, using a 2B, shade the bridge and the nostrils. You may follow the shading guides we looked at earlier. Keep in mind the importance of shading lightly and in small circles.

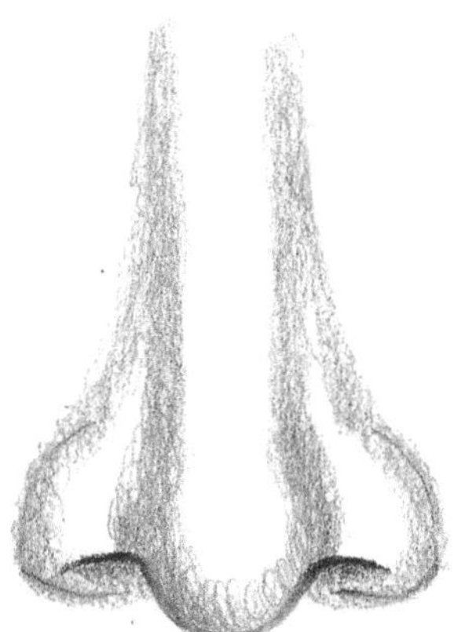

Step 5: Blend

In the next step, using a blending stump, blend the area that you shaded. When blending, use a circular motion to produce a smooth effect. Also, when blending the tip of the nose, follow the circle shape of it to create the illusion that it's protruding.

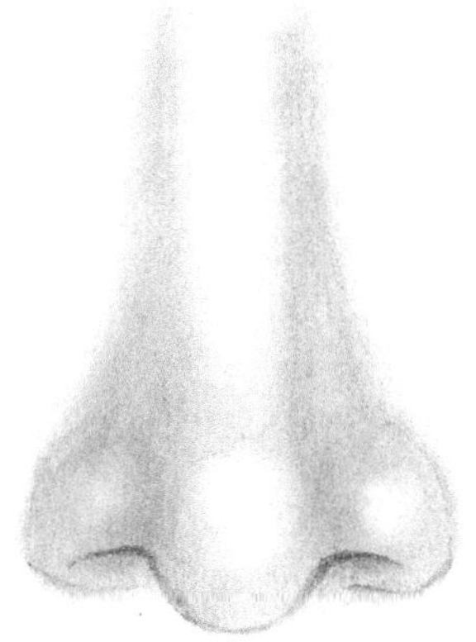

Step 6: More shading

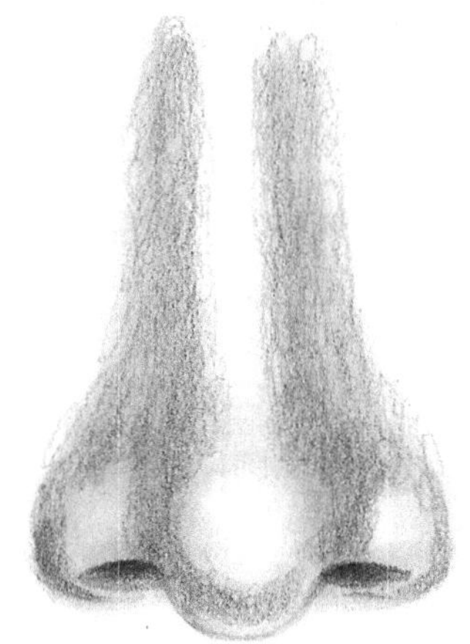

Using a 4B pencil this time, shade the parts that will be a bit darker. Take note of where the shadows mostly are. Again, shade in a small, circular motion. At this stage, you have most likely given the nose its shape.

Step 7: More blending

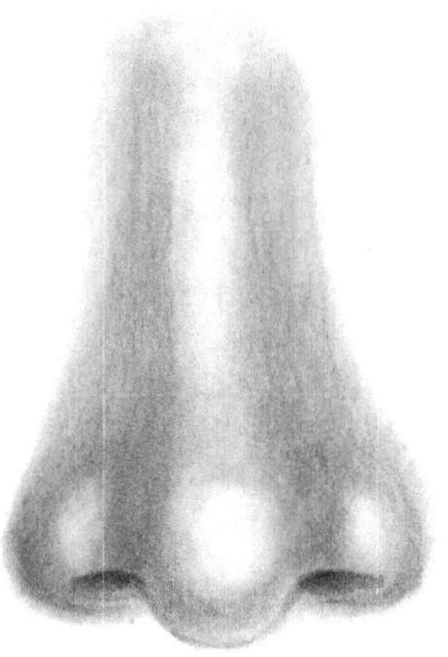

At this stage, you must blend the darker areas you shaded. Do not blend on the highlighted part.

Step 8: A bit darker shading

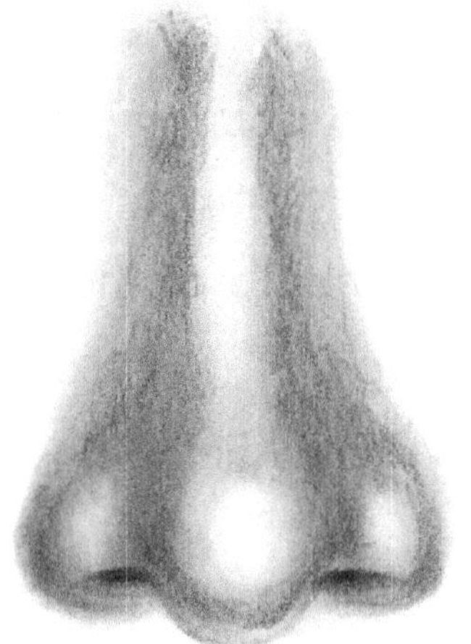

For this step, still using a 4B, try to apply a greater pressure to the page and shade the 2nd to the last darkest areas of shadow.

Step 9: Blend

Then, blend the part that you shaded again. Keep in mind to blend ONLY the part that you recently shaded. Keep the highlights untouched.

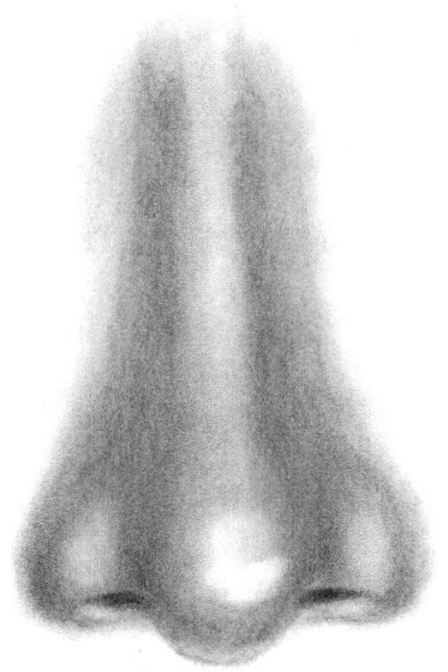

Step 10: Final shading

Now, using a 6B, you are going to shade the darkest area of the shadow. Don't press too hard, or it will be difficult to blend.

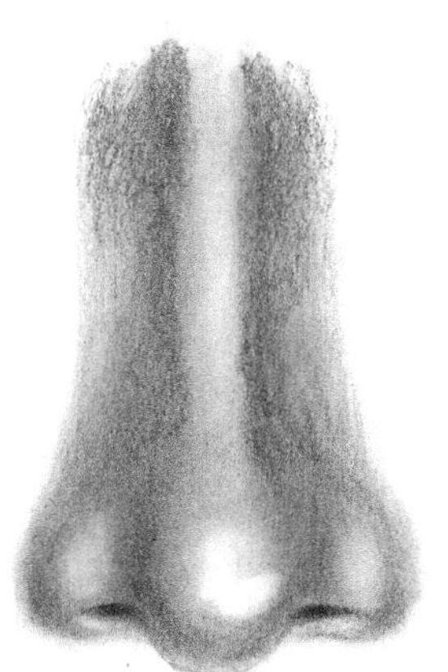

Step 11: Final blending

Finally, blend the most recent areas that you shaded, the darkest areas of the shadows, while still leaving the highlights untouched.

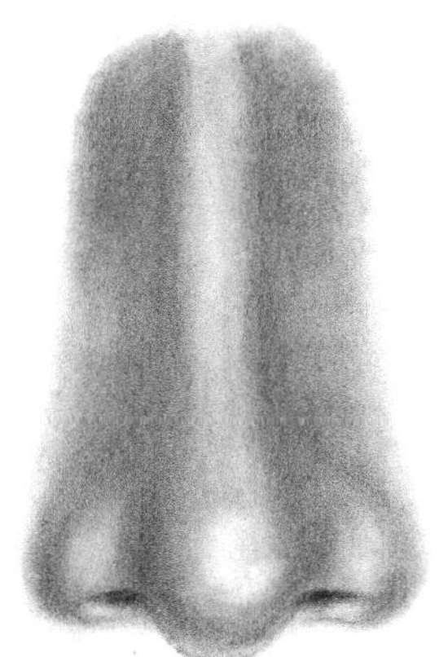

Step 12: Final outlines and highlights

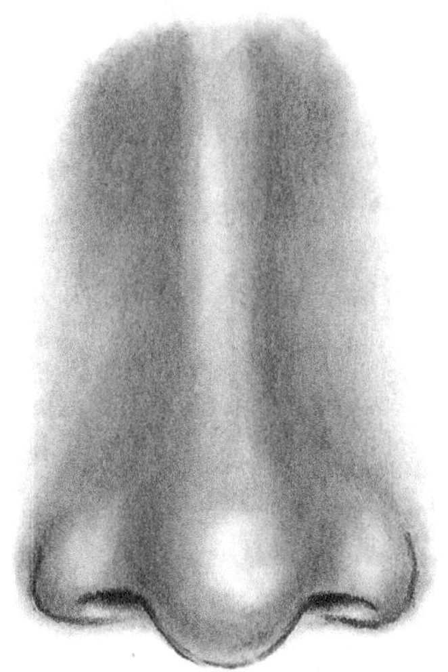

Now for the final step, using 4B or 6B, draw the outlines again to emphasize them. But make sure not to overdo this. Darken the hole of the nostrils using a 6B to finalize the look. Using a kneaded eraser, dab carefully on the nostril area and bridge where the highlight is. And as you can see, there is a part where the highlights look shiny. That is because we used the sharp part of the eraser for that. Do the same to give more detail to the nose and create an illusion of dimension.

Lips

If the nose is considered challenging next to the eye, the lips are the next most expressive element. After all, the eyes and the lips are what capture the emotion of a face.

Step 1: Draw the guidelines

Of course, we will start with the guidelines. For the guidelines of the lips, draw a horizontal line. Then above it, draw two overlapping triangles that are unequal, as you can see in the drawing above. Then below the horizontal line, draw a trapezoid. Draw this guideline using an HB pencil.

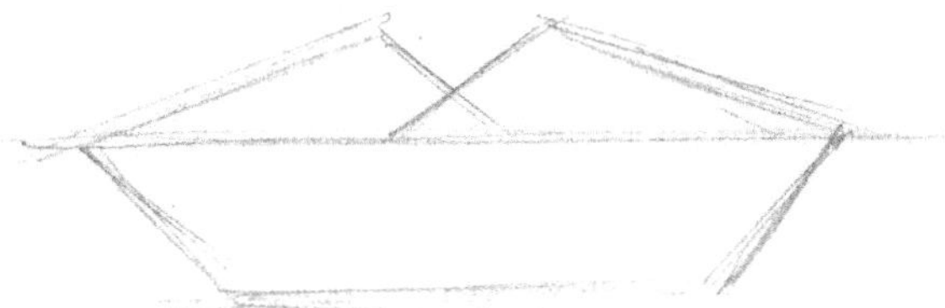

Step 2: Shape

From the guideline you made, using a 2B pencil, alter the shape of the lips according to your preference. The horizontal line is represented as the partition and opening of the lips.

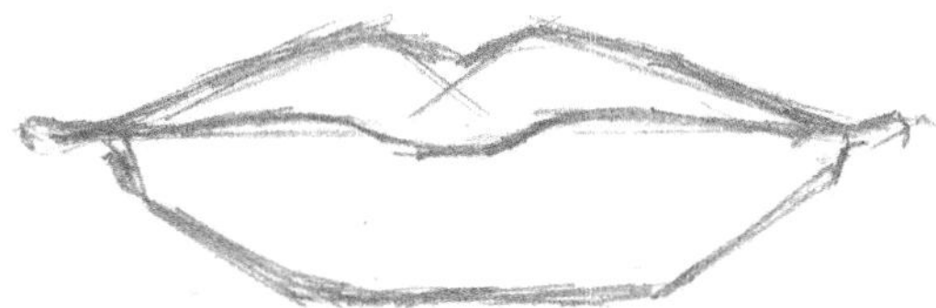

Step 3: Outline

Next, using the kneaded eraser, lightly erase the guidelines until you can just barely see them. These will still act as your guide in the steps later. Using a 4B pencil, finalize the outline of the partition of the mouth, which is the horizontal line.

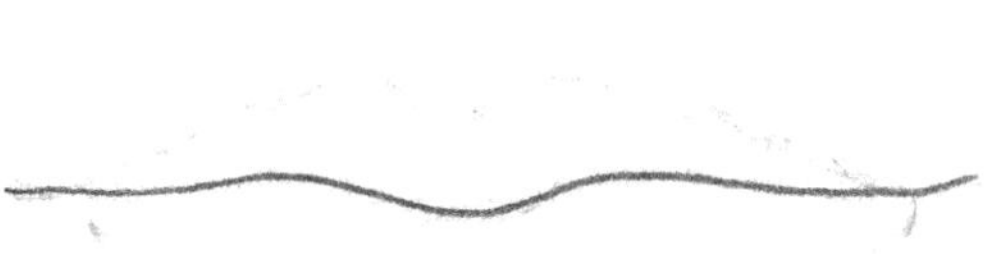

Step 4: Shading

Using a 4B pencil, start shading where the shadowed areas are. Don't make them too dark just yet. This will be the initial shading for the shadows.

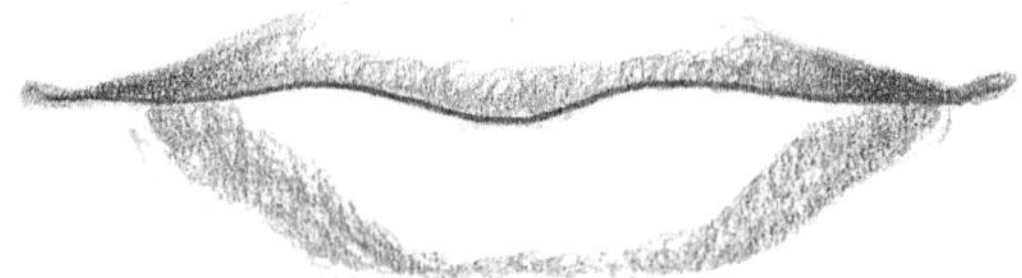

Step 5: Blend

Now, using a blending stump, blend the first areas you shaded. Blend in a circular motion without touching the highlights.

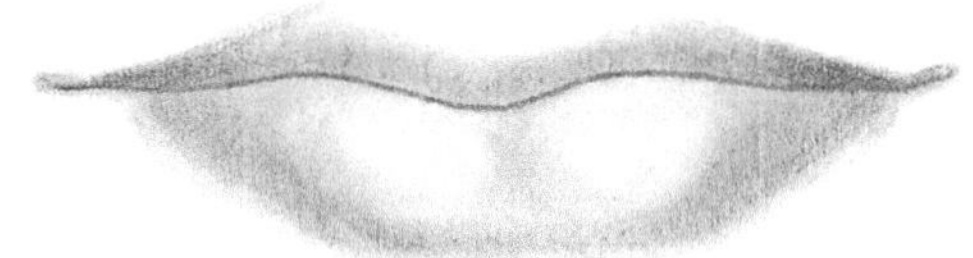

Step 6: Midtones

The next step is shading each lip in full using an HB pencil. Shade in one direction only.

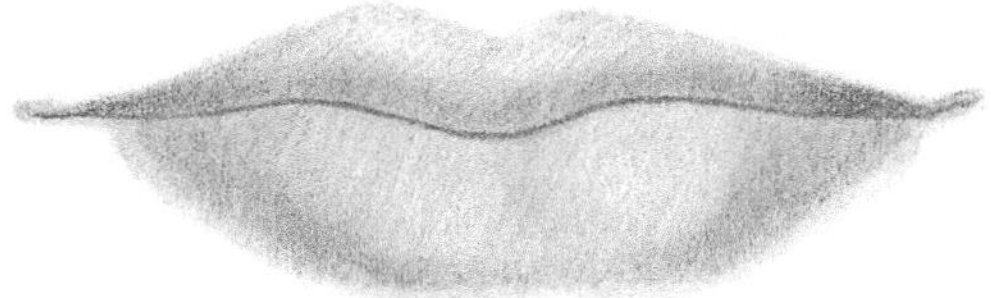

Step 7: Blend

Now, after shading and using a blending stump again, blend both lips. As you can see, even though you blended the whole area, the highlighted areas are still visible.

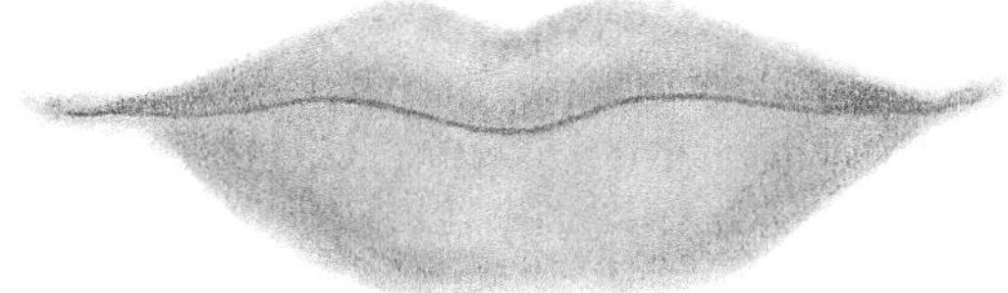

Step 8: Darkening the shadows

In the next step, using 6B pencil, make the horizontal outline of the lips darker. Then, using 4B, try darkening the shading of the shadows more. Using a 6B pencil, draw a shadow beneath the bottom lip. The shape of the shadow will depend on where you imagine the light source to be. Or, if you're using a reference, make sure you figure out where the light source is. Adding a shadow will make the lips look more protruding.

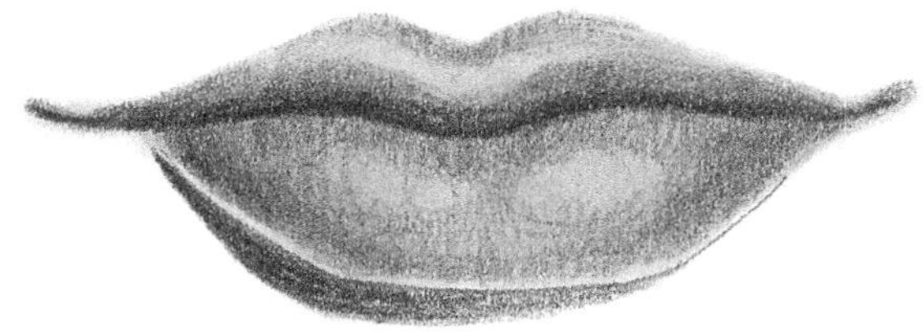

Step 9: More blending

As usual, in this step, you need to blend the recent parts that you shaded while still leaving the highlights untouched.

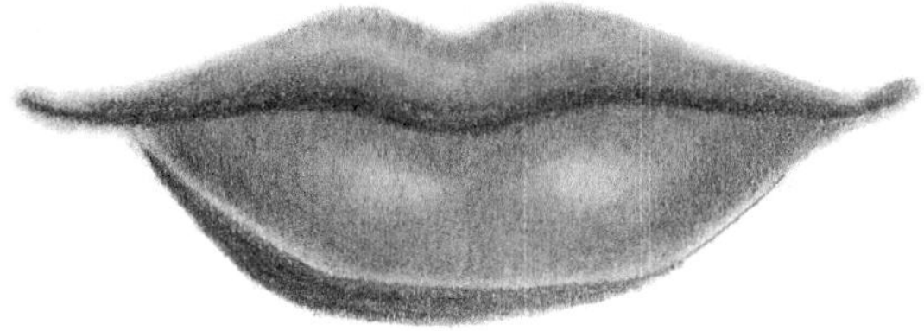

Step 10: Details

Now, using a kneaded eraser, dab carefully where the highlighted parts are. Then, using a 2B pencil, create lip wrinkles by drawing contoured lines on the lips. Make sure not to press too hard, as it will look less realistic.

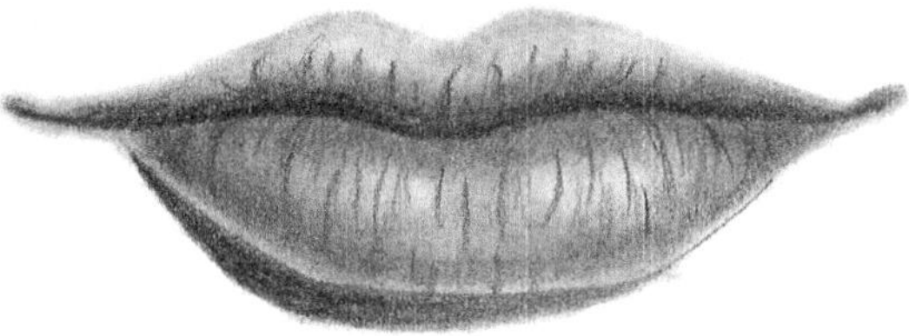

Step 11: Final blending

Smooth out the shading on the top and bottom lips using a blending stump. Avoid blending on the highlighted areas to make the lips look plumper. You'll notice that the wrinkles slowly start to blend in with the shading, but they shouldn't disappear.

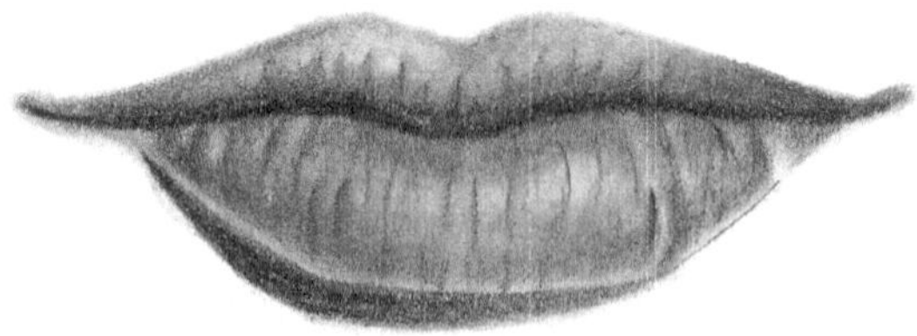

Step 12: Final details

Now to make the final details. Using a 6B pencil, darken out the areas that need more contrast and carefully blend them. Then, using a kneaded eraser, dab the highlighted parts carefully and add some highlights on the wrinkled areas to make them appear textured.

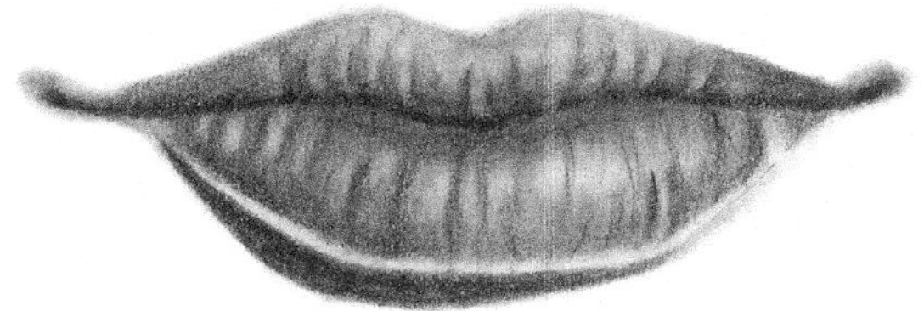

Ear

The ear may appear difficult because of its structure and folds, but let me tell you, it becomes a lot easier with the use of guidelines. These will guide you on where to shade and blend.

Step 1: Guidelines

For the ear, draw a rectangle. The rectangle will be the width and length of the ear, so draw according to your liking. Then, draw a diagonal line on the bottom right of it. Draw the guideline using an HB pencil.

Step 2: Outline

Using the guides you drew, start doing the outlines. This is the typical structure of the ear, so as a beginner, try and study these pictures to familiarize yourself with its parts. Every individual's ear has a unique shape, but we can still follow some general trends. Draw the outline using a 2B pencil.

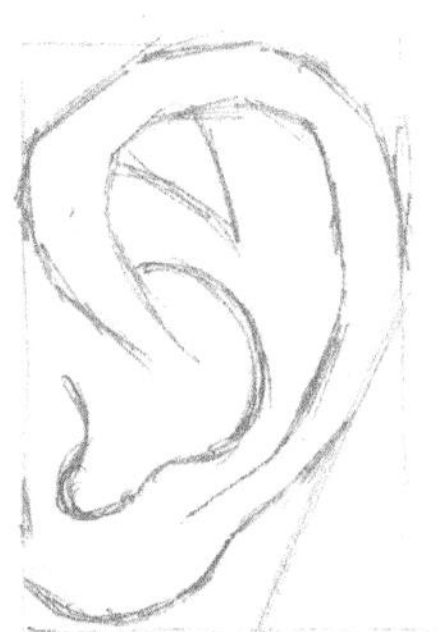

Step 3: Finalize outline

The next step is to erase the guidelines and then, using a kneaded eraser, carefully lighten the outline. You will now have a light, clean outline.

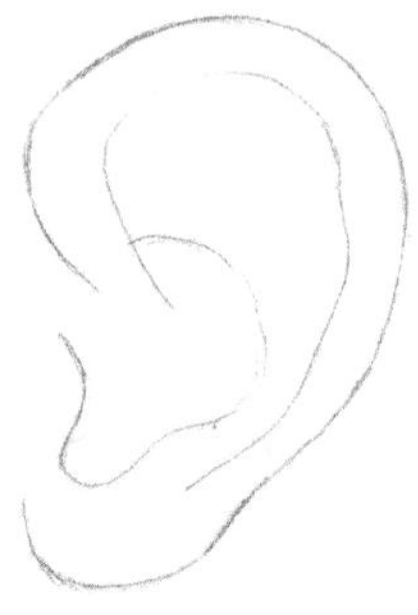

Step 4: Shade

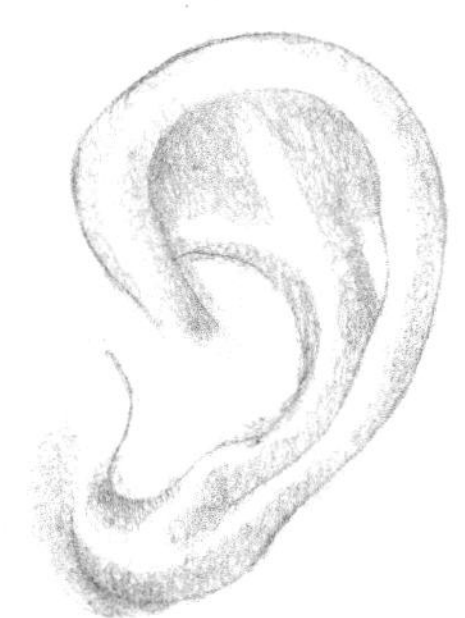

Using a 2B pencil, start shading all the parts with shadows. As always, we are shading the initial part of the shadow, so it doesn't have to be dark yet.

Step 5: Blend

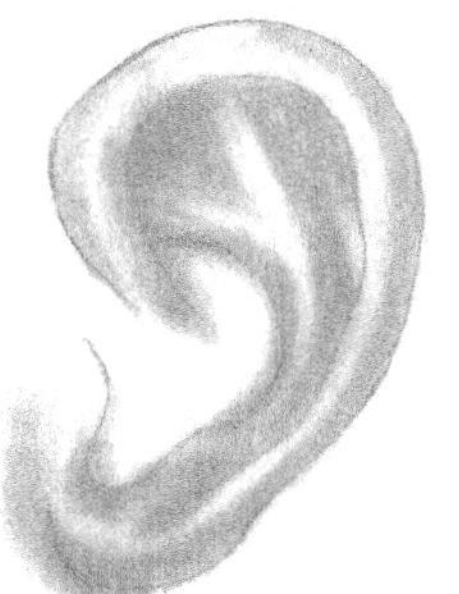

Now, blend the parts that you shaded and avoid blending in the highlights.

Step 6: More shading

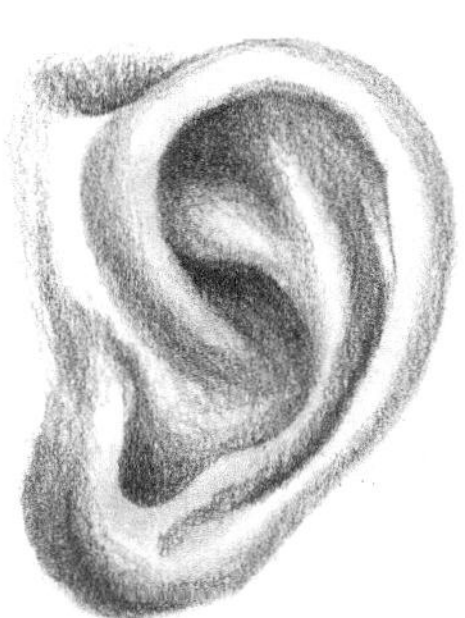

For this part, we are going to use a 4B pencil for shading the shadowed parts. We are now slowly building the value of the ear. Shade in a circular motion.

Step 7: More blending

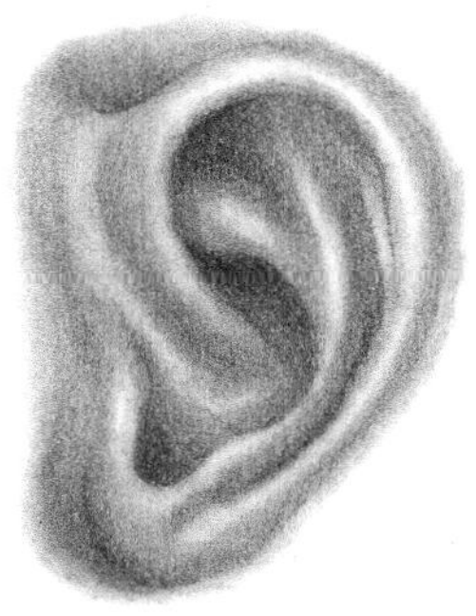

Then, of course, using a blending stump, blend the shaded areas, leaving the highlights alone.

Step 8: More dark areas

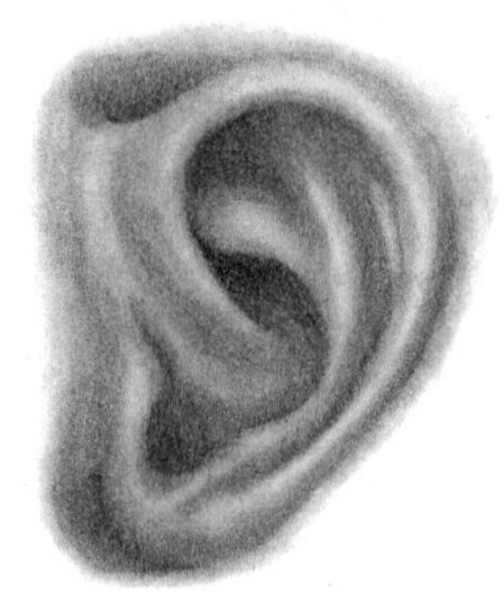

This time, use a 6B to emphasize the darker parts of the shadows and create more contrast. Thereafter, blend the areas you've shaded darker.

Step 9: Highlights

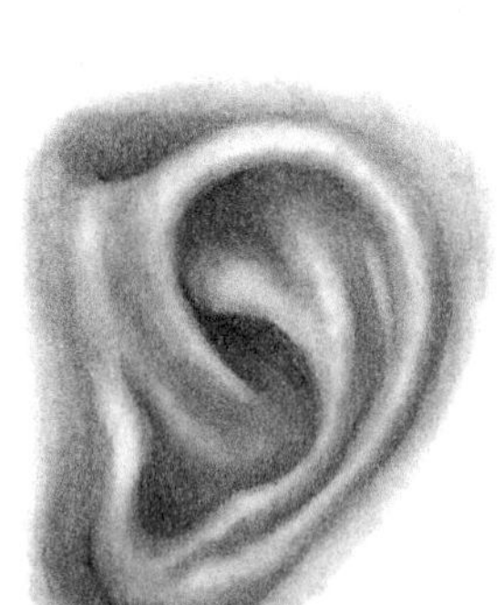

Emphasize the highlights using a kneaded eraser. Lightly dab it on the areas that are highlighted. Do not overdo this, or you might erase the shadow tone, which is difficult to fix.

Step 10: Final details

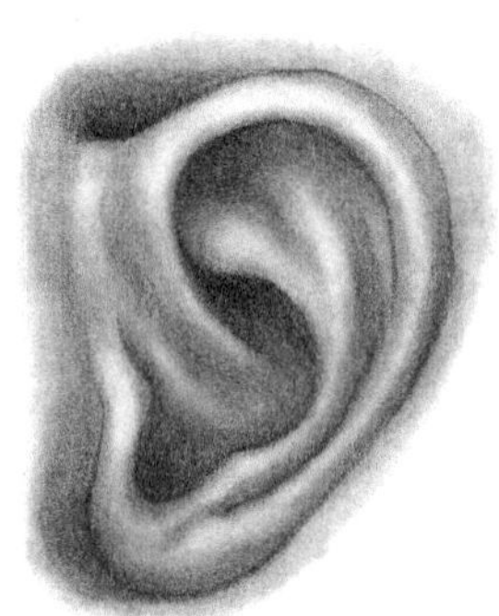

Using an 8B pencil, add a final darker shade to the shadowed areas and blend. Finalize the outlines using 8B grade as well. Keep in mind the guidance we gave before about outlines where light source is considered. You don't want your ear to look cartoonish by drawing a thick outline along the entirety of it.

Hair

For beginners, drawing hair is the most challenging part in a portrait, as well as the most stressful. This is because beginners think they need to draw each and every strand! You don't actually have to do that; there are various techniques that create the illusion of multiple strands of hair. Let's begin.

How to draw strands

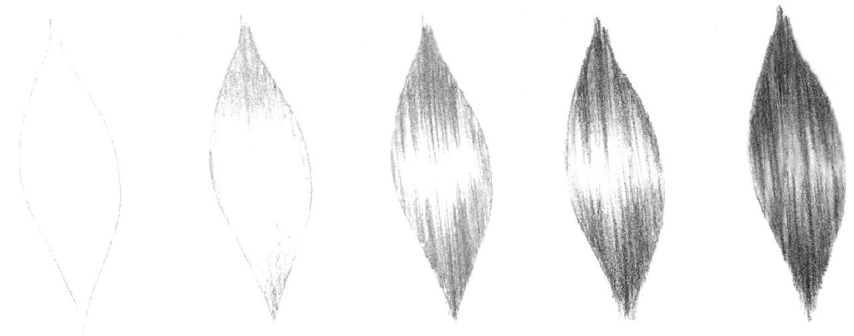

Here's an example of a small lock of hair to demonstrate how to draw strands.

Start by using an HB pencil or lighter if you prefer. Make light strokes on both ends. As you are making each stroke, remember to press and then lift as you approach the area you want to highlight. Work your strokes inwards so they fade in the middle of the lock.

For the second layer, use a 2B to make it a bit darker.

For the third layer, you can opt for a 4B and continue to build the value.

When you're happy with how it looks, finalize the details. Using a blending stump, blend the strokes inwards, leaving the middle shiny to represent the highlight. Then, finalize the highlight using a kneaded eraser. Just a few strokes will do. Don't overdo it, or else you might erase the whole thing.

Strands styles

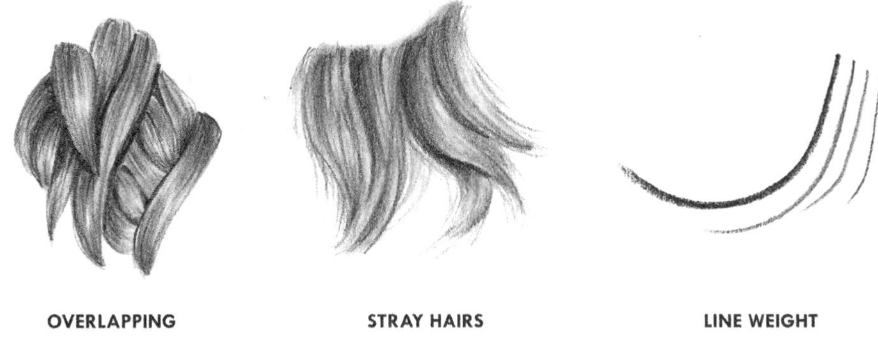

OVERLAPPING STRAY HAIRS LINE WEIGHT

Here are some more styles you can use when shading hair. Straight hair might seem easiest, but it isn't rewarding to always play it safe. Challenge yourself and make the hair in your portrait show more volume. Although, for beginners, it is understandable that drawing hair may seem difficult, practice will always be the key to improvement.

Curly hair

If simple, straight hair seems challenging, what about curly hair? Fret not, there are, and there will always be, techniques to draw these things with ease.

Here is a small lock of curly hair, for example:

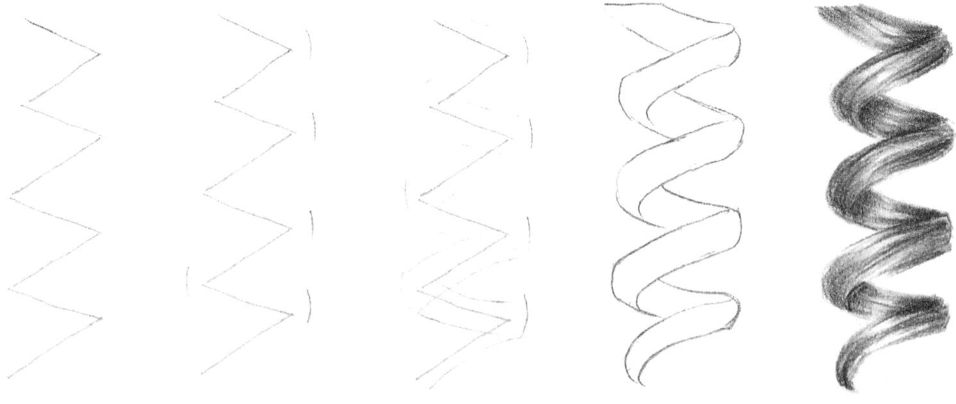

Draw a zigzag as guideline. This part depends on the kind of curl you are planning to draw, but for demonstration, we are going for the typical curl.

Next, draw vertical, curved lines on every corner of the zigzag.

Don't be confused by this part. On the first diagonal line, draw slightly convex curves on both sides. Then, at the next diagonal line, draw slightly concave curves on both sides. Thereafter, repeat the first step. You'll notice that they are in an alternate pattern. Do this until you reach the end of the zigzag. You'll see that the shape of the curl is slowly forming.

The next step is to erase the guidelines and fix the final outline. Make sure that the end of the curl is a pointed tip to indicate that this is the end of the hair.

Thereafter, draw the details with the same instructions as mentioned earlier. It's the same process, just a different style of hair.

Here's an example of a whole head of hair to show you how it will look:

Start by drawing the head shape and, from there, mark the hairline.

Draw the shape and outline of the hair you wish to draw. For this sample, I chose to draw medium-length hair with folds. You'll see later on how I shaded them.

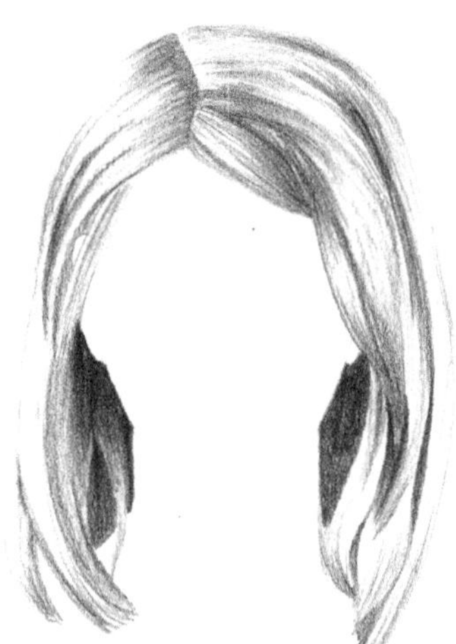

Once you have finalized the shape and style of the hair, erase lightly using the kneaded eraser.

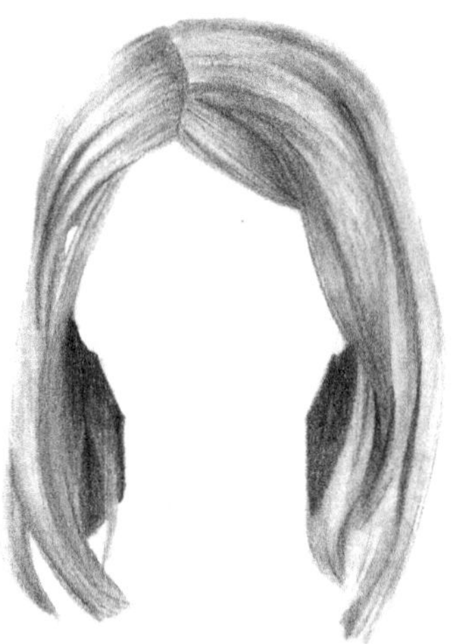

When doing hair, always start with the shadows. Yes, from dark, to mid, to light tones. This adds to the illusion of volume and creates value. These shadows will also serve as a guide for the whole shading stage.

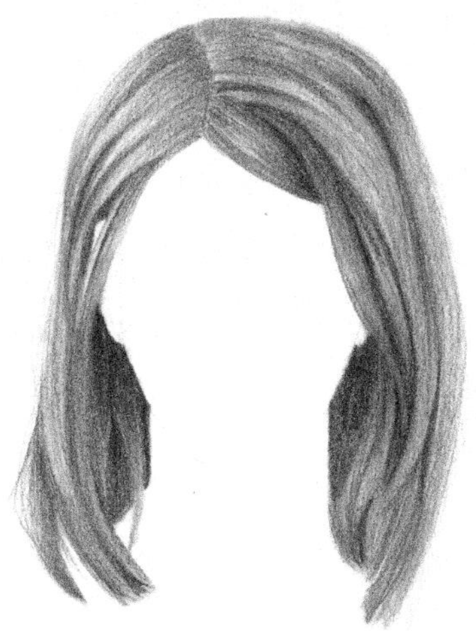

The next step is to blend it all. When blending hair, don't do the usual circular motion that we use for the facial features. Instead, blend using small strokes.

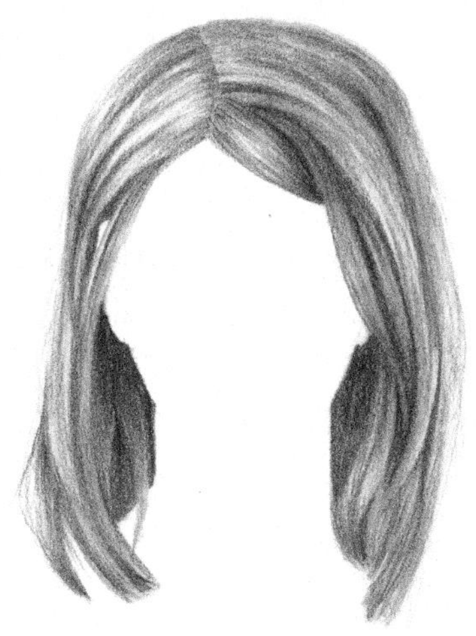

Repeat the process, but this time, darken the shadows. This will be the darkest area of your hair. Thereafter, blend the whole thing.

The final step is to emphasize the highlights using a kneaded eraser. Mold your kneaded eraser into a sharp corner to make thin strokes.

Practice makes perfect. As cliché as it may sound, it's the only way. At least now you know that you don't have to draw every single strand of hair!

Face Proportions: Male

Learn the basic steps in drawing the typical male facial proportions. For this process, use an HB pencil all throughout. You will only use a darker grade once you finalize everything, but as long as you might make more adjustments, use an HB or lighter grade. Let's get started!

Step 1: Draw a circle

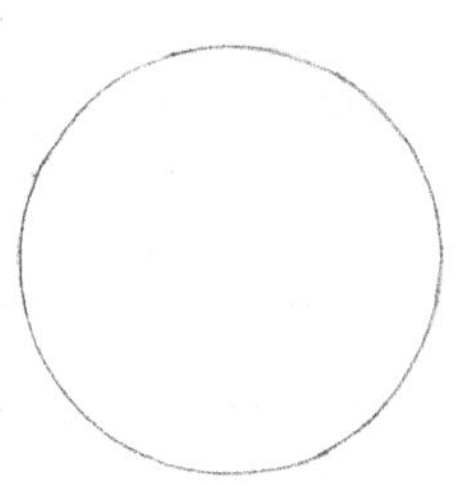

Start by drawing a circle. Don't worry too much about it being perfect - it's just a guide and will be erased later on. The important thing is that it's symmetrical. Next, draw a vertical line in the center from the top. The length of the vertical line outside the circle should be less that the length of the circle. They should not be the same size.

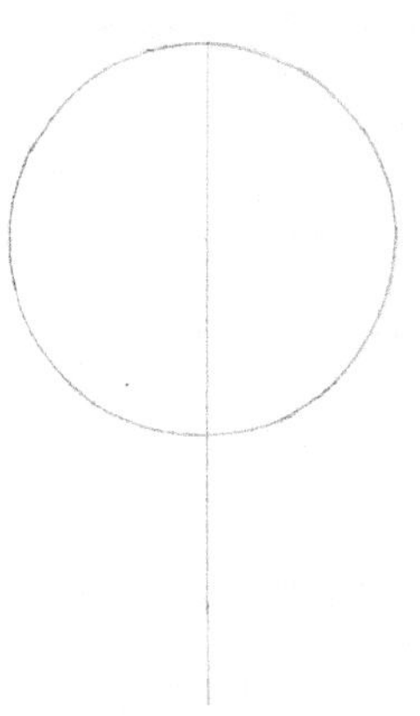

Step 2: Sketch the jawline

Draw a horizontal line under the vertical guideline. This will serve as the edge of the chin. Now, from the center side of the circle, sketch the jawline. Normally, a male's jawline is sharp and edgy compared to the smooth jawline of a female. Make sure the face is symmetrical.

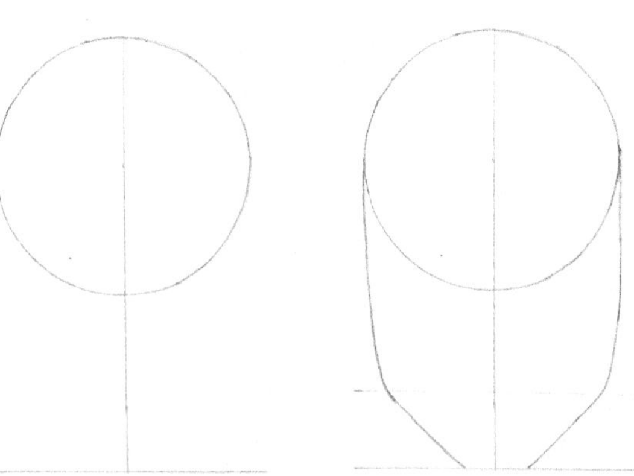

Step 3: Draw guidelines

The next step is to draw a guideline beside the face. Whatever the length of the face you sketched, divide it into eight. Now, the important guidelines here are 2, 4, 5, 7, and 8, so extend them horizontally. This will be the position of the facial features. Then, draw marks on the eye level, which is number 5 or the center line. Divide the width of your sketch into five. This will indicate the size and the distance of the eyes.

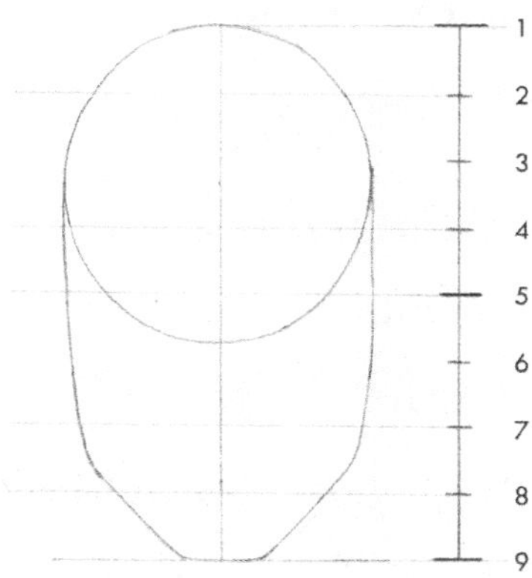

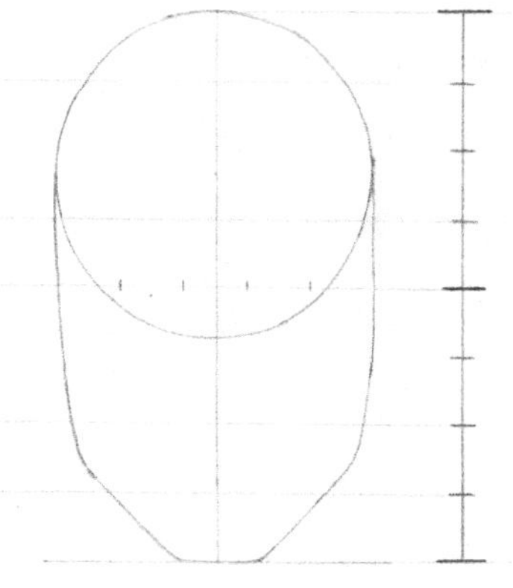

Step 4: Draw the eyes

From the guidelines you did earlier, sketch the eyes and make sure they're symmetrical. As mentioned earlier, the typical eye distance is equal to the vertical length of the eye. But remember that all eyes are different and unique. We are just following the typical dimensions so that we have something to follow. Now, from the tear duct of the eye, draw vertical lines downward. This will serve as the guideline for the nose.

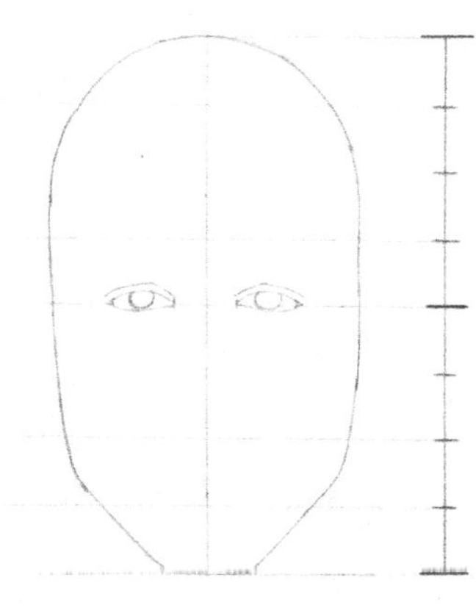

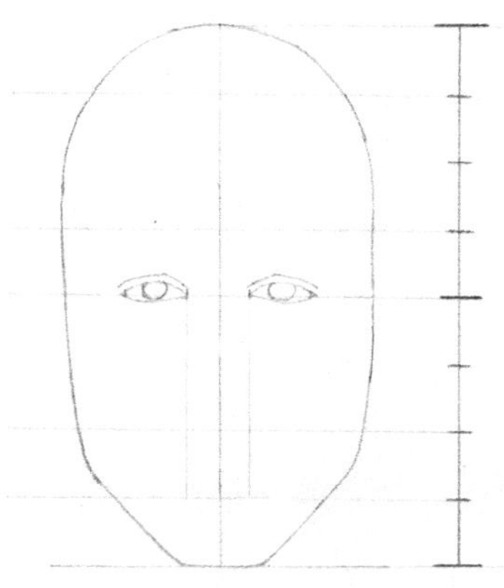

Step 5: Draw the nose

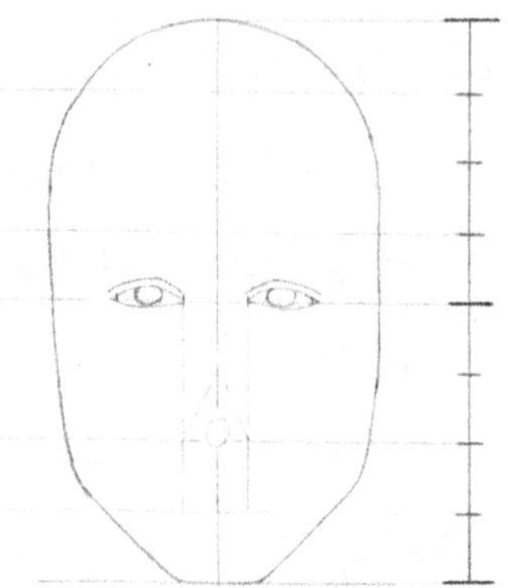

The next step is to draw the guidelines for the nose. These particular guidelines were discussed in an earlier topic. So, if you remember, this is how the guidelines should look. After that, define and finalize the shape of the nose. Make sure not to draw the bridge of the nose because that will be mostly shading, although I did indicate a mark here just to show where the bridge of the nose should be.

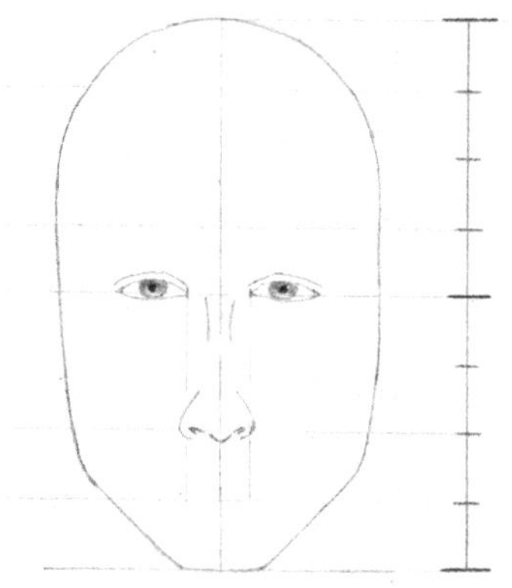

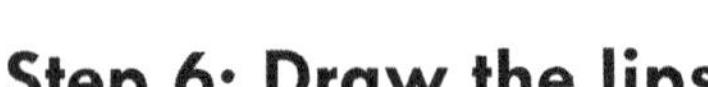

Step 6: Draw the lips

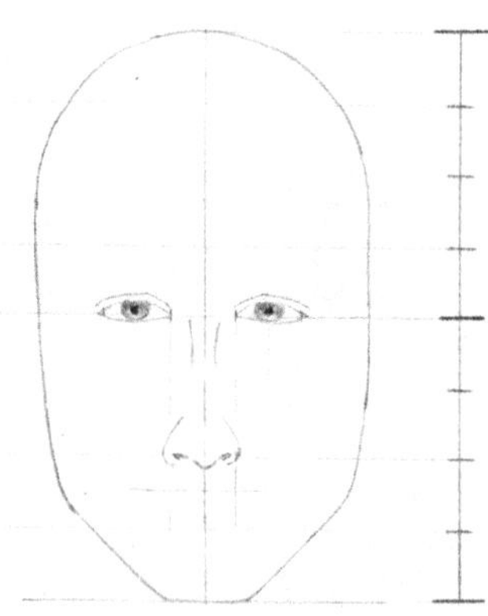

Now that we have the nose for this sketch, let's move on to drawing the lips. From the center of the eye, draw a vertical line downwards. This will be the edge of the lips. Again, for the lips, draw the same guidelines as we did on the topic solely for lips. This is how they look when placed on a portrait.

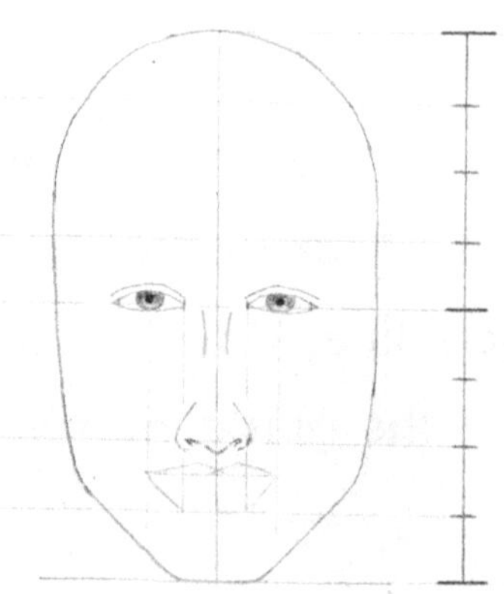

Step 7: Sketch the eyebrows

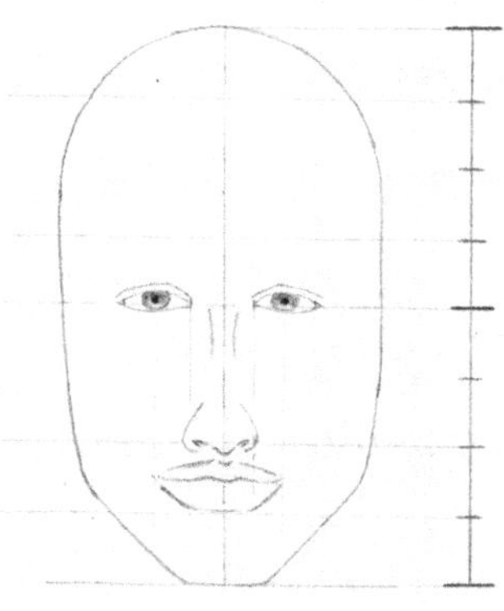

After drawing the guidelines for lips, it's time to define them and give them shape. It's up to you how you'd like the lips to look, but normally, a male's lips are much stiffer and straighter than a female's curvy ones. Now that the lips are finalized, let's move on to the eyebrows. As you can see, I drew a diagonal line upwards to the corner of the eyes. This will indicate the curving line of the eyebrows. You can draw any shape you prefer, but for males, the eyebrows are usually quite thick.

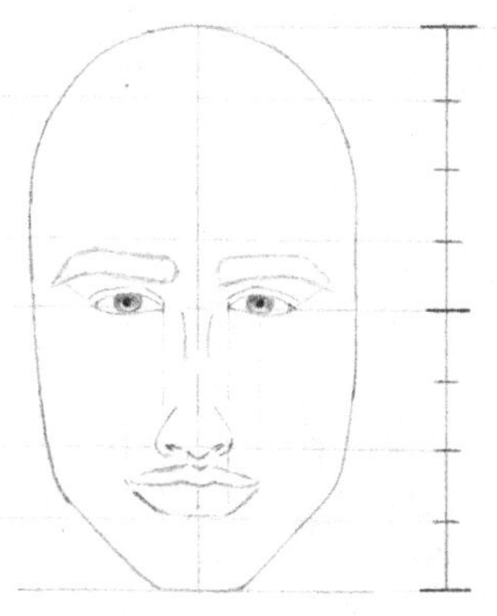

Step 8: Draw the rest of the features

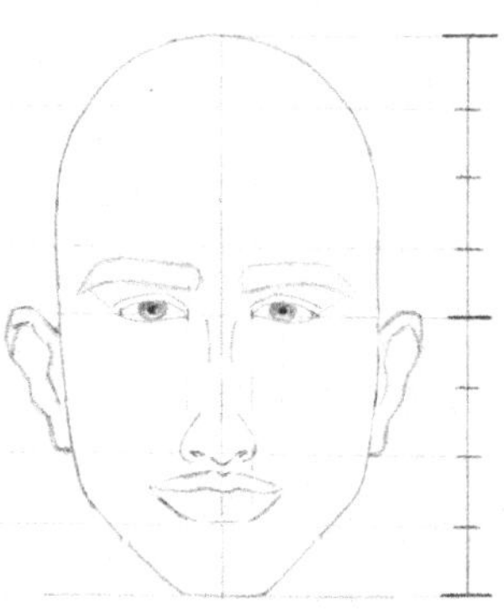

To determine the length of the ears, use the center line 5 to line 7. However, this also depends, as, like I said earlier, every human's face and proportions are unique. Now, for the hair, draw the hairline between lines 1 and 2. For a receding hairline, make sure you are above line 1. Don't place it exactly at line 1, as this will make your face look odd. Shape the hair

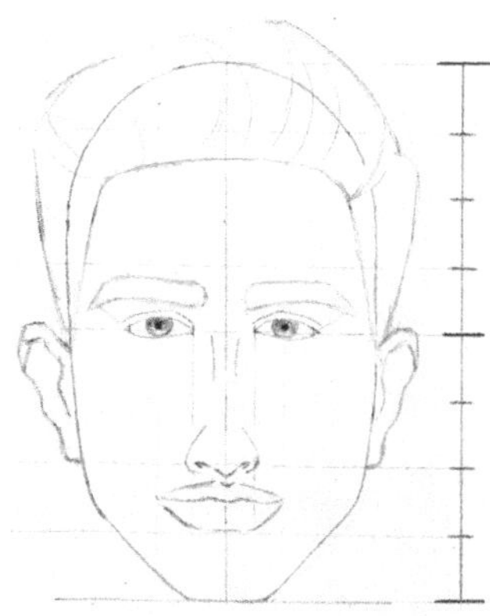

according to your preferences and add guidelines for later on.

Step 9: Finalize

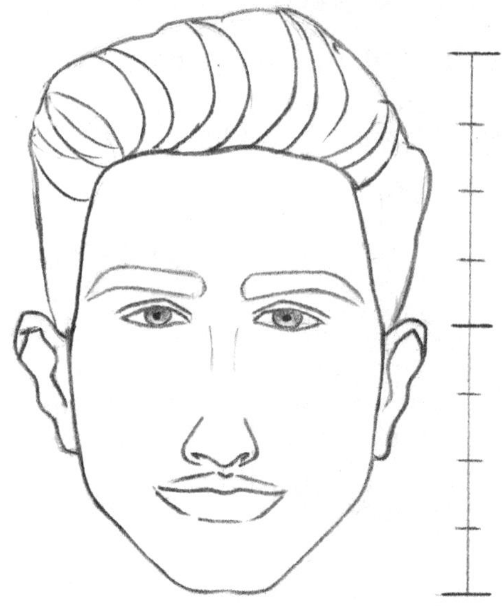

If you are satisfied with everything, carefully erase the guidelines using a rubber eraser. It's much better if you use the pencil eraser so as not to mess with the other lines while erasing. Then, add fine details. Notice that I made the chin more masculine. I then added contours on the hair to make the portrait look like it has a specific hairdo rather than just the outline of the hair.

Always remember that every man's facial features and proportions are unique and different. So, for practice, try to observe pictures of men and do a proportion study.

Face Proportions: Female

For this topic, you are going to learn the basic steps in drawing a female face. This is similar to the first face proportions we did, only this time, it's a female face, so there are a few small changes. We are going to talk about that as we go along. Remember to always use an HB grade and light pressure for this process, as you are only going to use a darker grade when it's time to finalize your drawing. Alright, let's start.

Step 1: Draw a circle

Of course, we will start with a circle. It doesn't matter if it's not a perfect one. Keep in mind that this is just a guide, but keep it clean and workable. Draw a vertical line in the center. The line outside the circle should be half or almost haft of the diameter of the circle. Usually, females have shorter chins and jawlines compared to males. So, a longer, sharper jawline would create a masculine look.

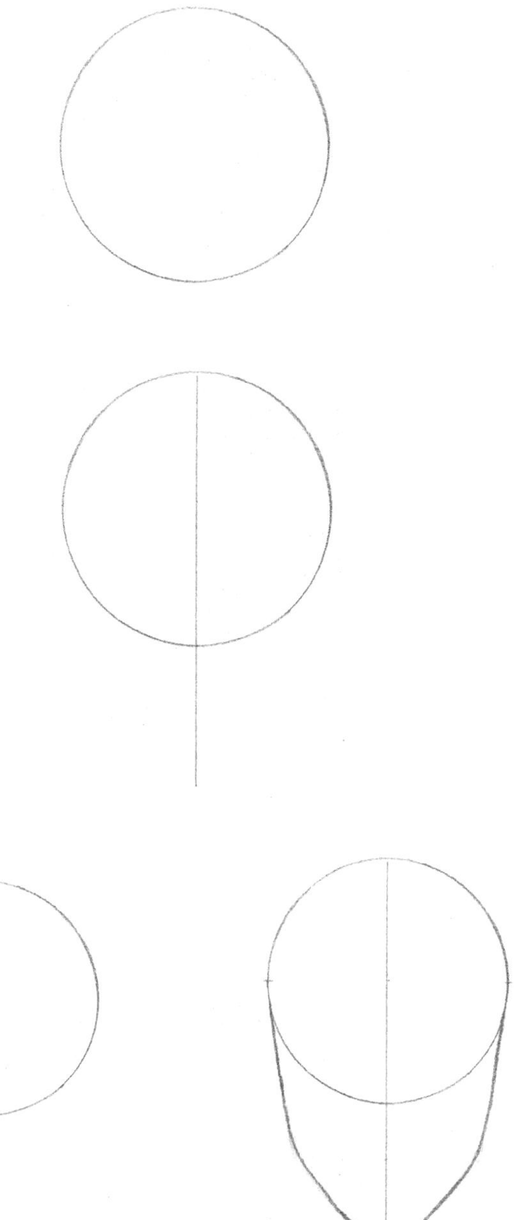

Step 2: Sketch the jawline

Now draw a horizontal line beneath the vertical line to serve as guide for the chin. As I mentioned above, females usually have smaller and softer edges compared to males. Draw the jawline, starting from the center half of the circle.

Step 3: Draw guidelines

Now, measure the length of the face you've sketched and divide that into eight. Label the lines and remember the important ones; they are numbers 2, 4, 5, 7, and 8. They are going to be the position guides for the features of the face. Next, on the center line, which is the line number 5, draw ticks and divide them into 5 equal parts. These are going to be the guidelines for the eyes.

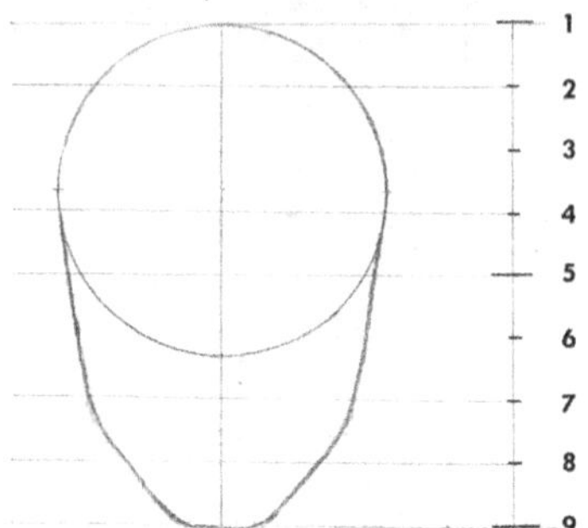

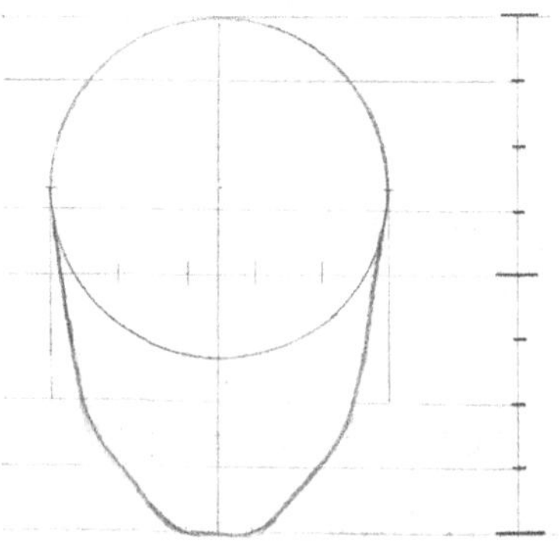

Step 4: Draw the eyes

Now that you have measurements for the eyes, sketch them. Always remember that female eye features are usually wider and softer. Draw them according to your preference. Next, draw vertical lines extending from the corner of the eye's tear duct to the line number 8.

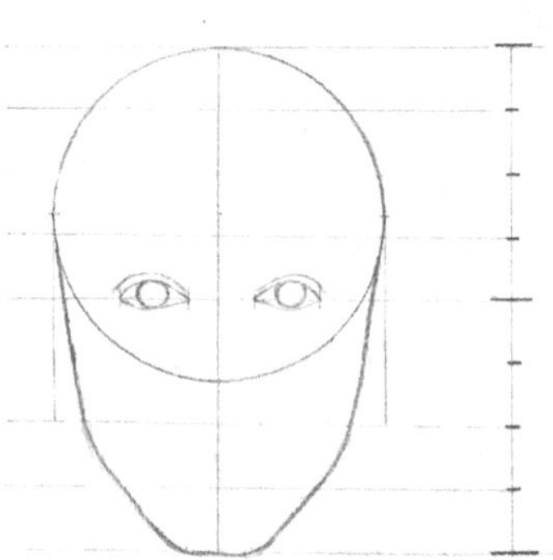

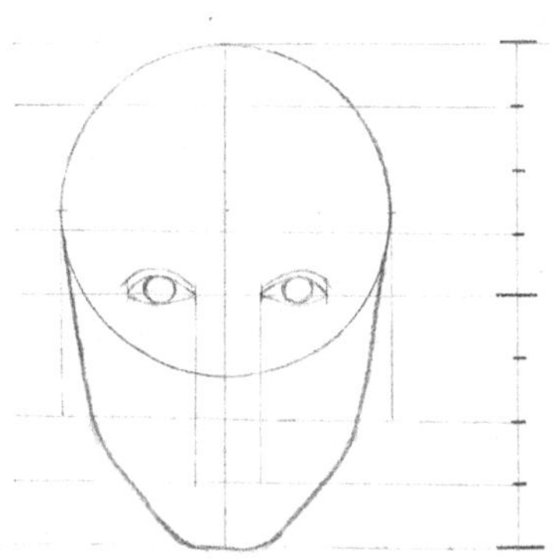

Step 5: Draw the nose

Use the guidelines for the nose that will serve as its width. Sketch the guidelines first, then finalize the shape of the nose while keeping in mind the soft features. And, as I always say, draw only the nostrils, because the bridge of the nose is done by shading.

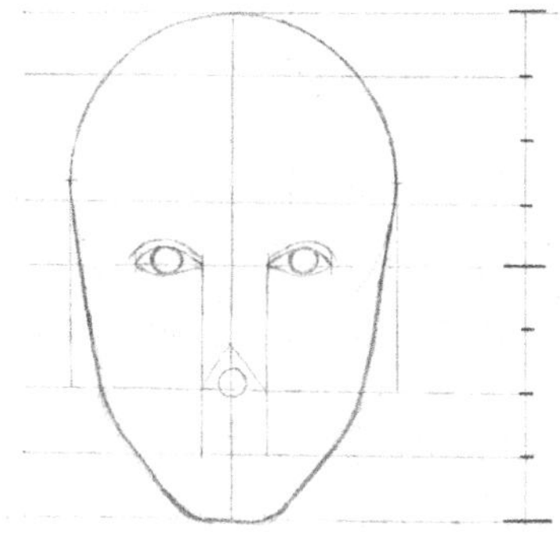

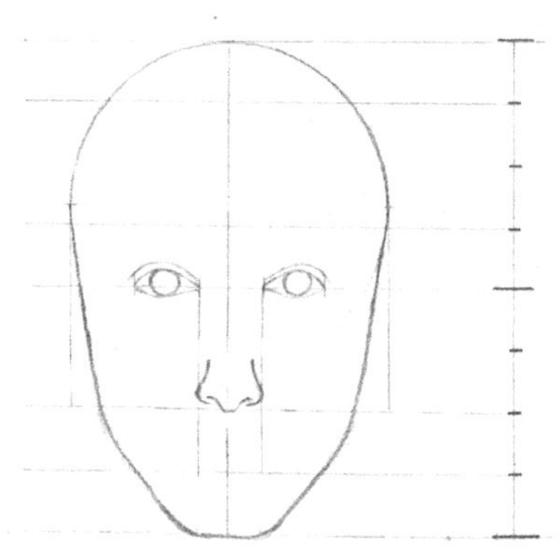

Step 6: Draw the lips

As for the lips, draw a vertical line from the center of the eyes extending to the line number 8, where the lips will be drawn. Then, draw a horizontal line between lines 7 and 8. This will be the partition of the lips. The distance of this guide depends on the shape of the lips you want to sketch. As for this example, I placed it a little bit higher than half. Next is to draw the rough guidelines for the lips.

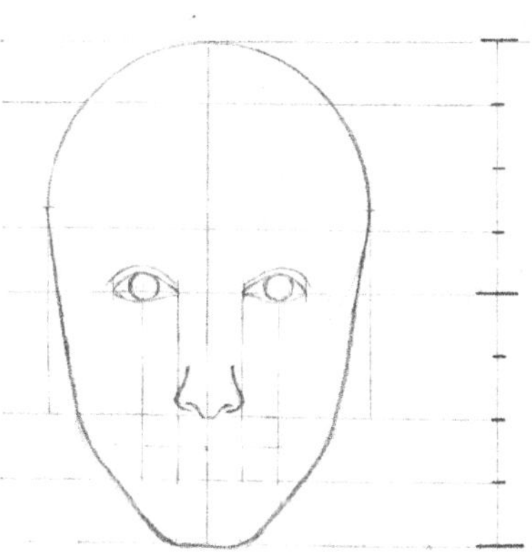

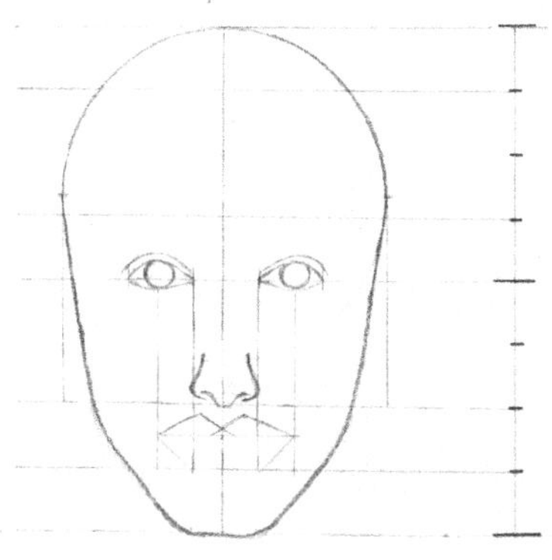

Step 7: Sketch the eyebrow

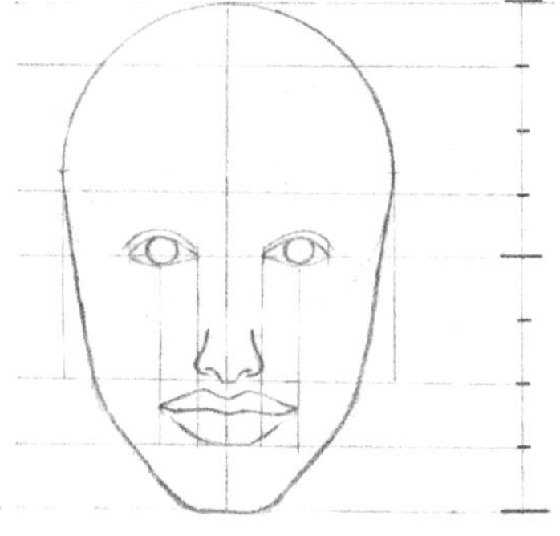

Finalize the shape of the lips according to your liking and, when you are satisfied with them, move on to the eyebrows. Female eyebrows are usually slender, longer, and sharper at the end than males'. As you can see in the drawing, we used a diagonal guideline to determine the concave curve of the eyebrows.

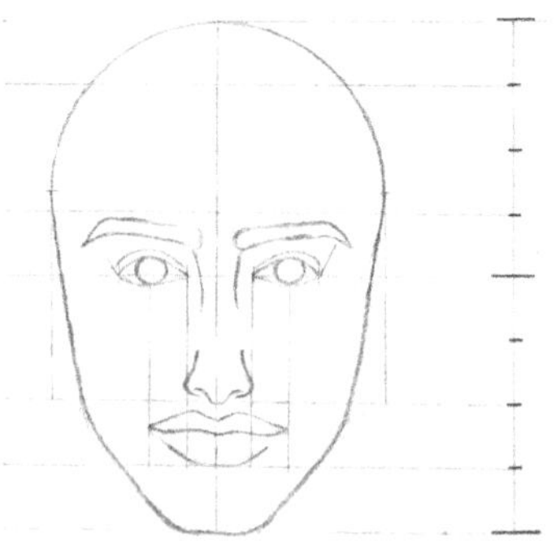

Step 8: Draw the ears and hair

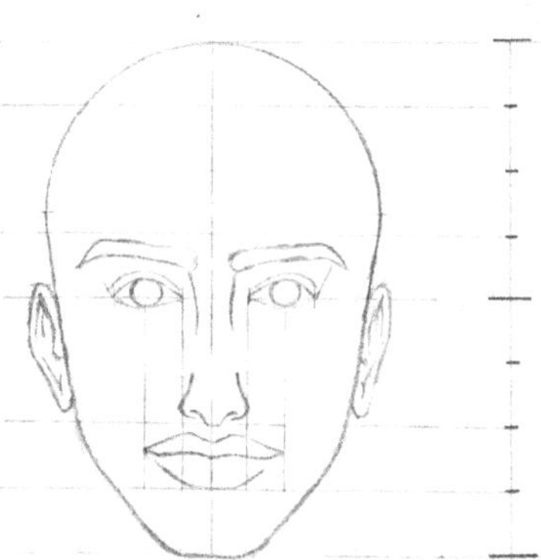

To draw the ears, make sure you don't go beyond line number 7. However, you can go a little bit above line number 5 or the center line, although this all depends. Every face is unique, so there are some faces with smaller, larger, or longer ears that might go beyond the measurements you just followed. Nevertheless, for the example, let's stick to that rule. Now the exciting part - doing the hair. You can draw the hair in whichever style you like. You can think of yourself as a stylist! Just make sure that, when drawing

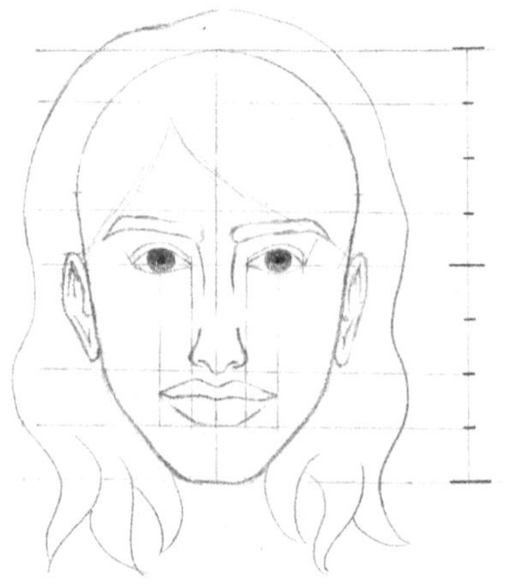

the hair, you go beyond the lines when sketching the outline so it looks more realistic.

Step 9: Finalize

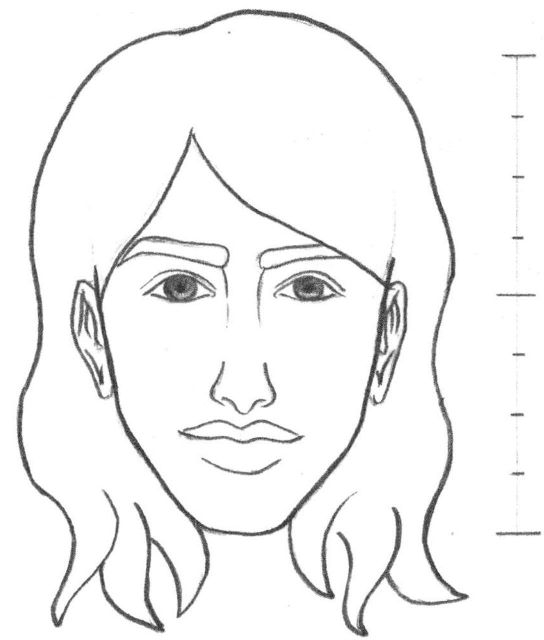

Now, if you are satisfied with every feature, you can use a darker grade to finalize everything. If not, you can still make adjustments. Don't worry too much about spending a long time adjusting things. It's normal, and even intermediate artists and experts do this. What's important is that everything is proportional. Also, if you'd like to make major changes to the features, you may do so. Take your time and always keep in mind that everybody's features are unique!

Face Proportions: Children

Children's proportions are different from an adult's. Since they're still growing, their faces are smaller, and their features are not yet fully developed. Here is the step-by-step process for a child's facial proportions.

Step 1: Draw a circle

The base will be a circle, as always. Once again, do not fret if the circle is imperfect, as it is just a guideline. Try your best, however, to make it symmetrical. Thereafter, draw a vertical line in the center. The line beyond the circle should be ¼ of the diameter of the circle. This is because a child's face is shorter and still not fully developed.

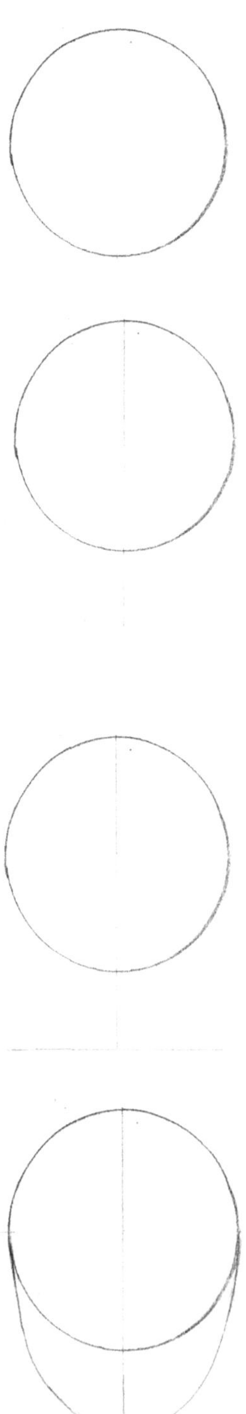

Step 2: Sketch the jawline

Draw a horizontal line just under the edge of the vertical line. This will serve as the length of the whole head from the top edge of the circle. Then, from the center side of the circle, slowly but surely sketch the jawline. Children's jawlines are usually round, unlike with adults, whose facial features are already sharp and edgy. Also, their forehead is usually wider compared to a fully-grown adult's head.

Step 3: Draw guidelines

The guidelines for a child's head are different from an adult's. First, draw the center line of the circle. Then, divide the bottom part into 4 equal sizes. These will be the guidelines for each feature. 1 is the for top of the head. 2 is where the eyebrows will sit, although a little bit below the line. 3 is for the eyes, 4 is for the nose, 5 is for the lips, and, lastly, 6 is for the chin. Now, on the line number 3, divide the horizontal line into 5 equal parts. This will be the length of the eyes and the distance between them.

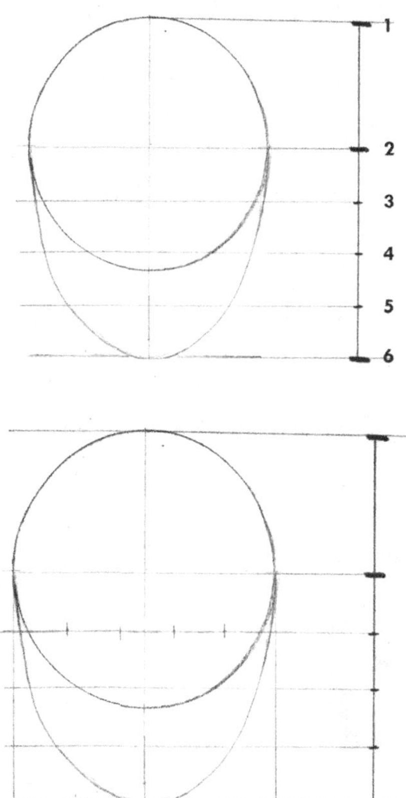

Step 4: Draw the eyes

The eyes of children are usually large and round. They are larger than the rest of their features because eyes are fully developed at birth. Now, for the nose, draw a line starting from the inner corner of the eyes. This will be the length of the nose.

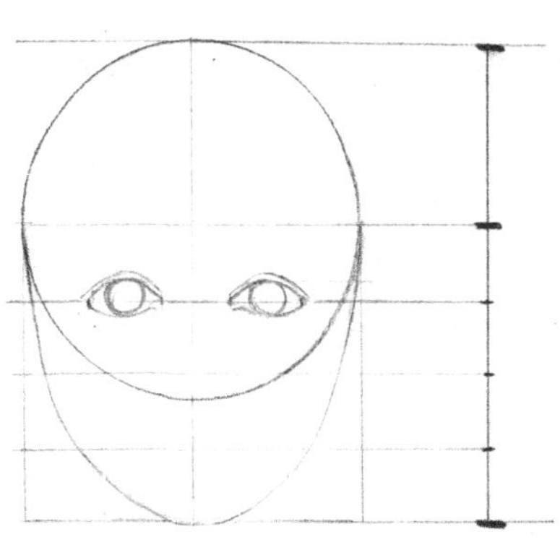

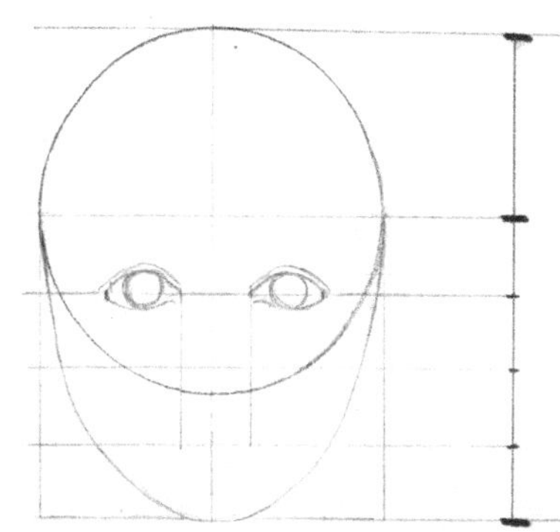

Step 5: Draw the nose

Following the usual steps, draw the guidelines for the nose in the same way as was discussed in the previous topic. As you can see, the child's nose is closer to the eyes. Almost all the features are closer to each other on a child's face. Thereafter, finalize the shape of the nose however you prefer. Make sure to only draw the outline for nostrils because the rest of the nose is shaped through shading and blending.

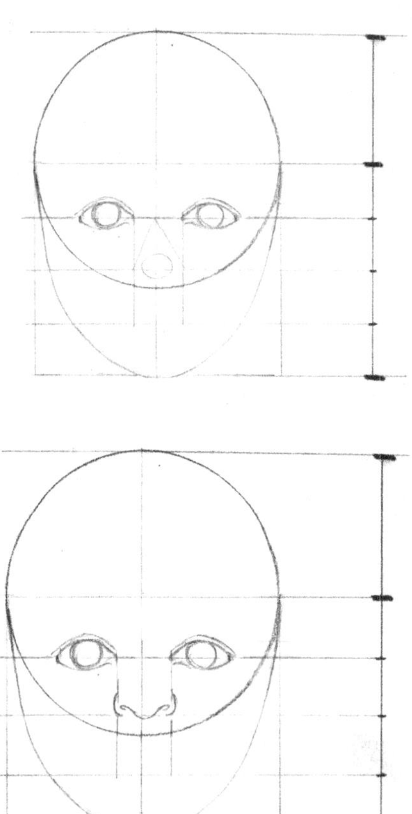

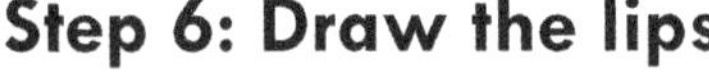

Step 6: Draw the lips

As for the lips, extend a line from the center of the eyes. This will serve as the edge of the lips. Then, draw a horizontal line between guidelines 4 and 5. Finally, sketch the guidelines for lips as shown above. Keep in mind that this may differ according to your liking. This is just a guide to help beginners draw these features.

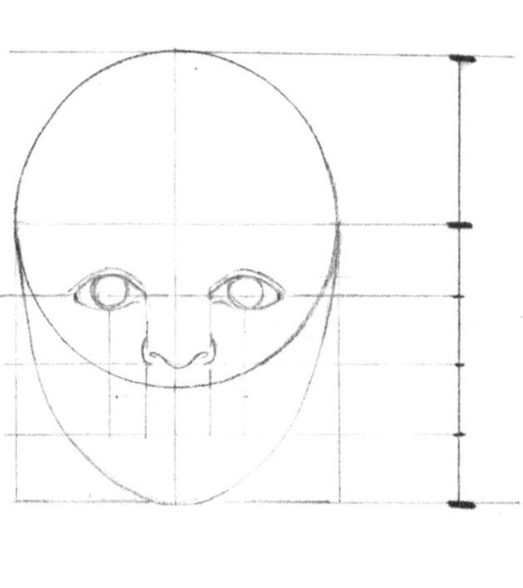

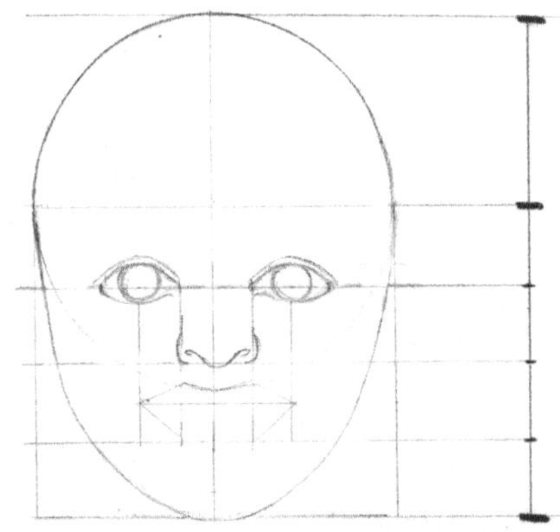

Step 7: Sketch the eyebrows

After drawing the guidelines for the lips, it's time to finalize them. Now for the eyebrows. They will be drawn a bit under line number 2. Normally, they are thin, as the rest of the hair is still growing.

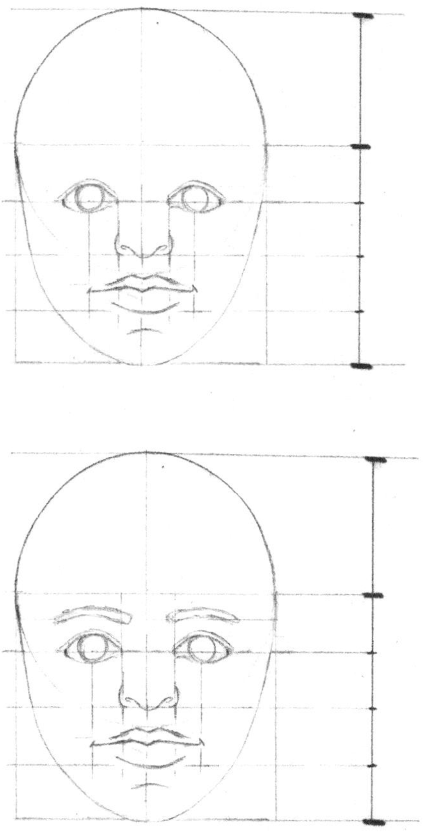

Step 8: Draw the ears and hair

The ears usually sit on guidelines number 3 and 4. You can play with these guides because everybody's features are different. Now for the hair. Again, you can play with wherever you want to place the hairline. Keep in mind, however, that a child's forehead is normally wide and becomes smaller as they grow up, depending on their genes. Make sure that the outline of the hair is above the circle guideline so it will look realistic and not cartoonish.

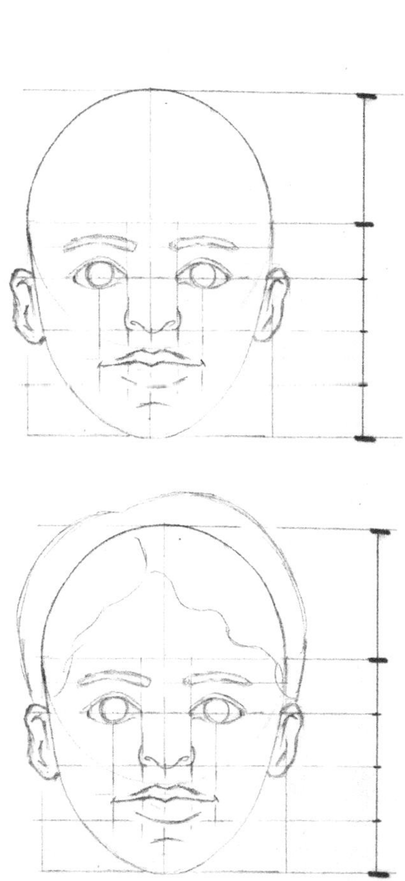

Step 9: Finalize

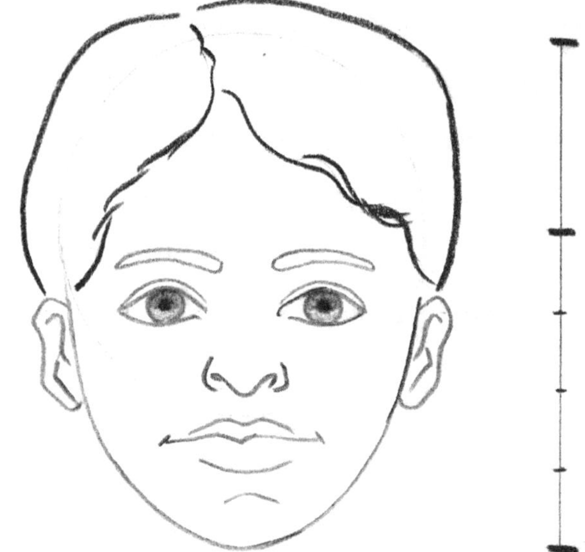

Remember that you can always adjust and erase if you are not satisfied with some features. That's why you should not use a darker grade during the first stages of the process. Keep in mind that every person's face is different and that every feature is unique. So, you have the choice to play around with some of the features while still following the standard guideline.

How to Draw: Front View

There are plenty of methods and techniques for drawing a head from scratch. In this topic, however, we are going to tackle the famous "Loomis Method" by the master illustrator, Andrew Loomis. His method is very popular among artists, be they beginners or not. This is because his method is easy to learn and remember and can be applied to drawing any angle of the head.

The method and guidelines are easy to follow, but it still takes practice and patience to achieve a successful face drawing. Always keep in mind that minimal progress every day is better than none.

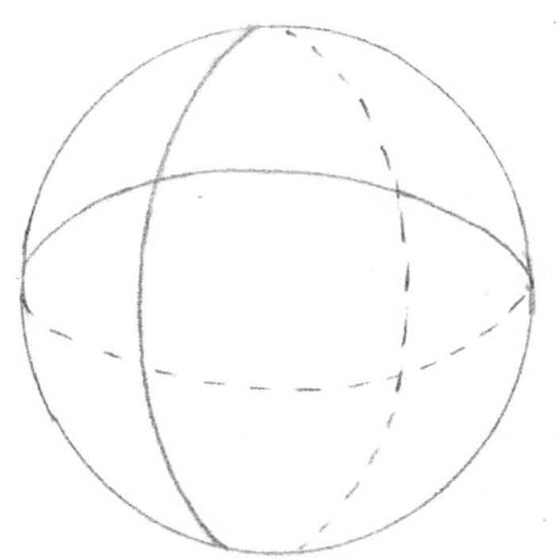

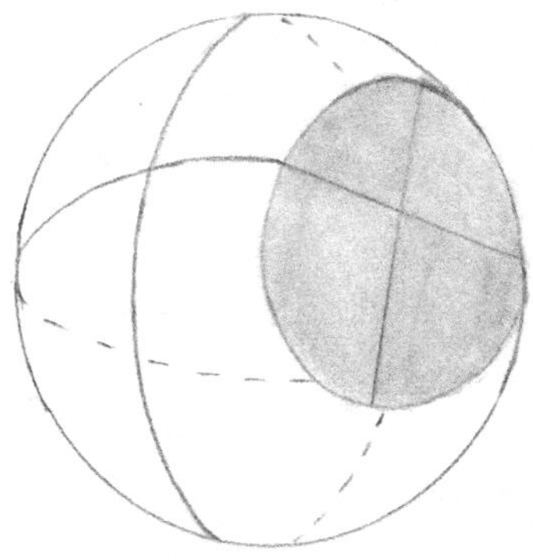

The concept of the Loomis method is simply drawing a sphere. Thus, the first step is drawing a circle. We then place our guidelines to give the circle dimensions and make it look like a sphere. Now, imagine slicing off the side of the sphere. The above illustration shows how this will look. That example is actually a head facing slightly upper left, but the good thing about this method is that it still works for flat angles like the front and side view. For this chapter, let's begin with the front view.

The very first step is to draw a circle. It doesn't matter if it's not perfect, as long as the length and width are equal. Next, divide the circle into 6 equal parts.

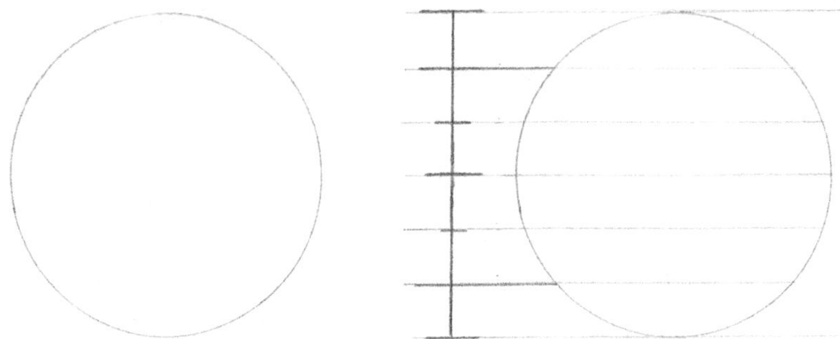

Now, chop off both sides by drawing curves from the inside on both sides. The length of the chopped part is two thirds of the length of the circle. On the second illustration, you'll see that I drew another curve from the outside to make the chopped-off part thinner and more realistic.

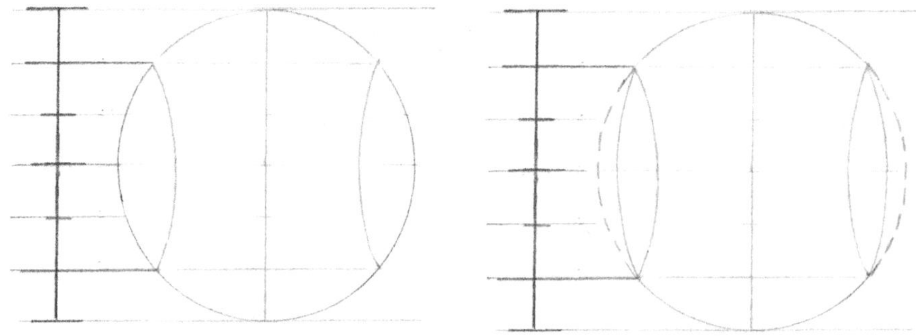

This is how the final shape will look. The sphere will be thinner now that the sides of the circle have been trimmed. For the next step, draw a line in the middle of the circle. That is where the brow is going to be. The middle of the circle is actually a third of the eventual face. The bottom line indicates where the bottom of the nose should be placed. The same length from the brow line to the nose line should be measured below the nose line to place the bottom of the chin. The line at the top can be used as a guideline for the hairline.

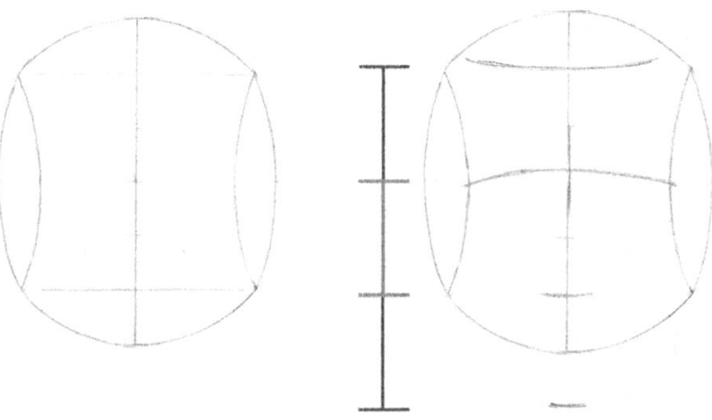

Now, attach the jaw to the bottom of the trimmed part. Draw it at an angle because a person's jaw is thinner at the bottom. Indicate the size of the chin and, finally, complete the shape of the jaw.

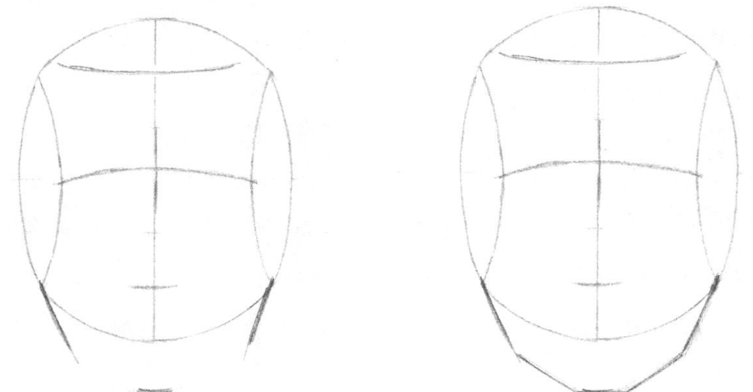

Complete the centerline and add the neck. The neck usually starts at the starting point of the jaw as well. The center guideline is only applicable when the view is front facing. The ears are normally at the middle thirds of where the brow guideline is placed and ends at the end line of the chopped curve. In other words, the earlobes should be in line with the bottom of the nose.

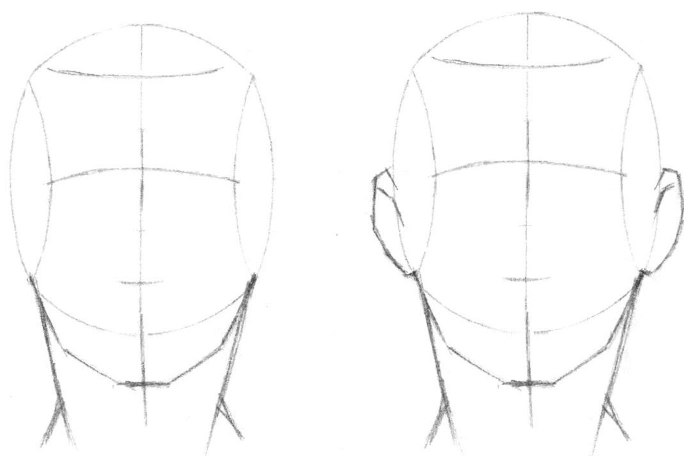

The final step is to establish each feature. The center line of the circle is where the eyebrows sit. The line below it, as we established, is the bottom of the nose. The guideline between the line for the nose and the chin is where the lips sit. You can play around with these features since everybody's face is unique, but you have to remember these standard proportions, as these are the basics.

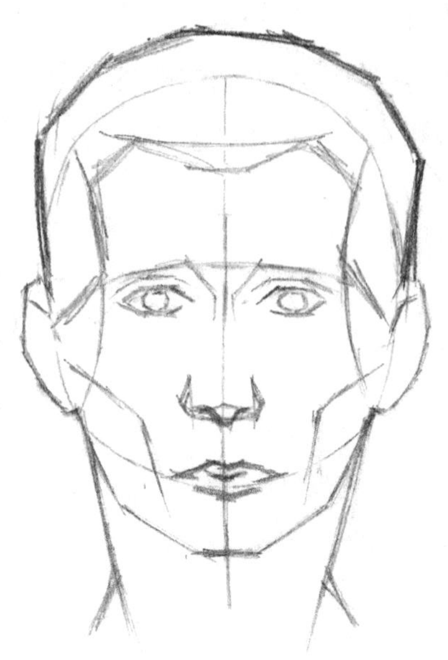

How to Draw: Side View

For this view, everything's the same. If there are differences, they are few and far between. The concept is still the same and we are still on the flat angle for this view.

For a side view, draw a circle with equal dimensions and draw another circle inside. The dimensions of the inner circle are two thirds the size of the outer circle. Then, draw a cross as a guideline inside the inner circle.

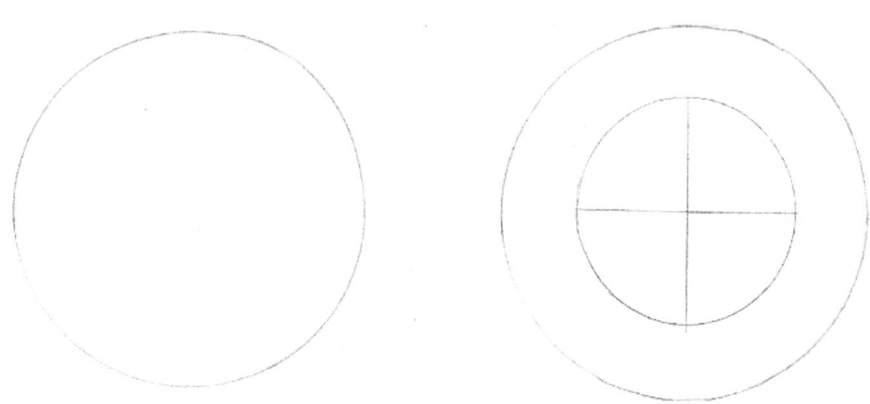

Next, extend the horizontal lines from the center and bottom of the inner circle to the edge of the outer circle. These will be the guidelines for the eye and nose respectively. Thereafter, measure the distance between the bottom edge of the inner circle and the bottom edge of the outer circle. Draw a line below the bottom of the outer circle the same distance away. This will be the guideline for the chin. Next, slowly establish the face by drawing a curve from the center of the inner circle to the chin part, and on the other side, a straighter one for the jawline also connecting to the chin. The curve may vary from person to person, but this illustration is the standard.

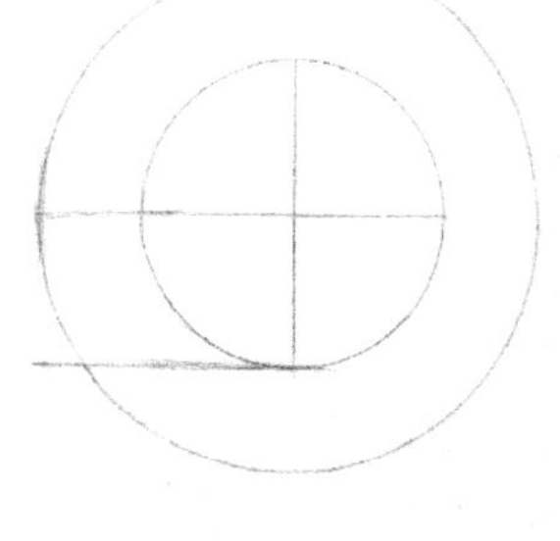

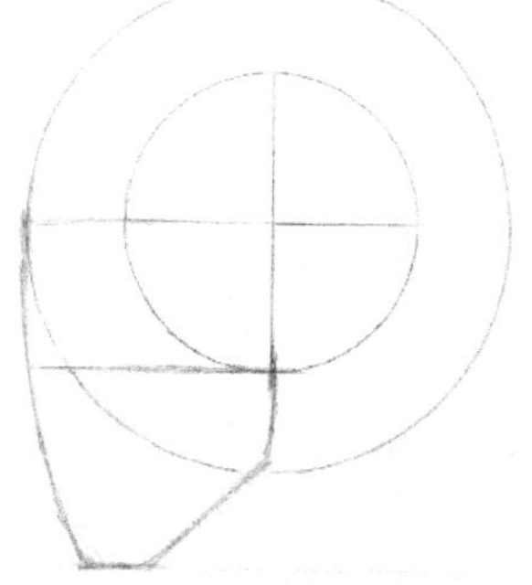

Slowly build up the jaw and the neck. Drawing the side view is much easier than the front view because it doesn't require as much detail. It's more important to establish the structure of the face. I suggest studying and observing portrait pictures that are facing sideways so you'll have an idea of how the structure of the face is formed.

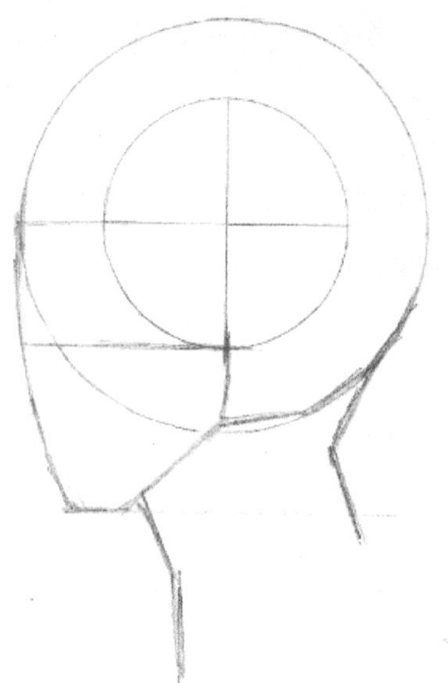

The final part is to build the rest of the details, the features, and the hair. It may be challenging to draw the features at a side view if you have been practicing mostly on front view. I recommend you use a reference so that you have a better understanding of how to draw the features sideways. Also, always remember when drawing the hair to go beyond the circle guideline.

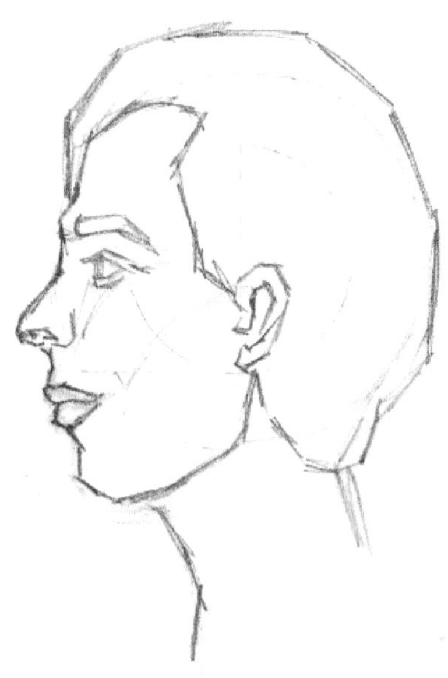

How to Draw: ¾ View

The "Loomis Method" is the most basic and effective approach to learning how to draw a head. For this guide, we are going to draw a ¾ view. Let's get started.

The first step is to always draw a circle. It doesn't have to be perfect, but make sure it's symmetrical. Divide the diameter by 6. This is all going to make up your guidelines.

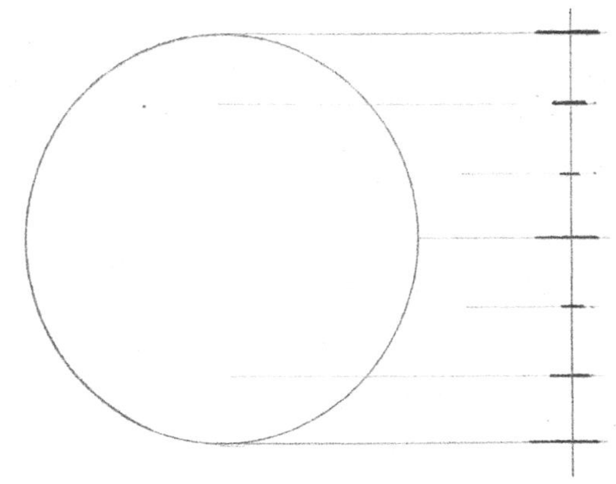

The tricky part will be drawing the oval. The height will always be the same, no matter what angle you're drawing the head from. It occupies $^2/_3$ the height of the circle. To get this in a simple way, use the 2nd and 5th sections as your guidelines for the oval. It may take time to perfect drawing the oval, so always be patient. The width and location of the oval will depend on the direction in which the person is looking.

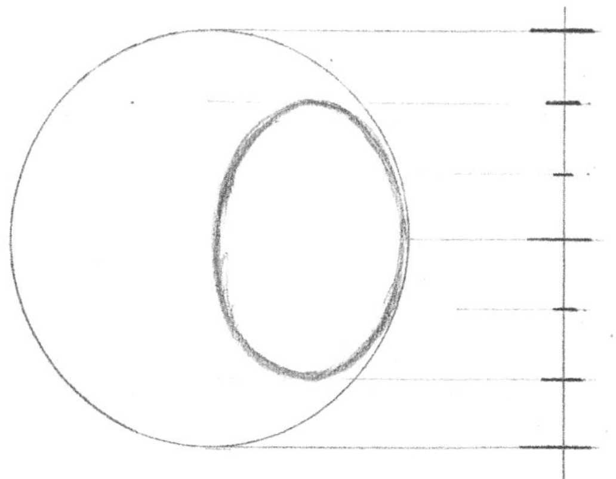

The tilt of the head is indicated by a horizontal line in the middle of the oval. As for our drawing, it is slightly tilted up. If the head is tilted down, then the line should be tilted downwards as well. This horizontal line is the angle from the ear to the brow. Keep that in mind.

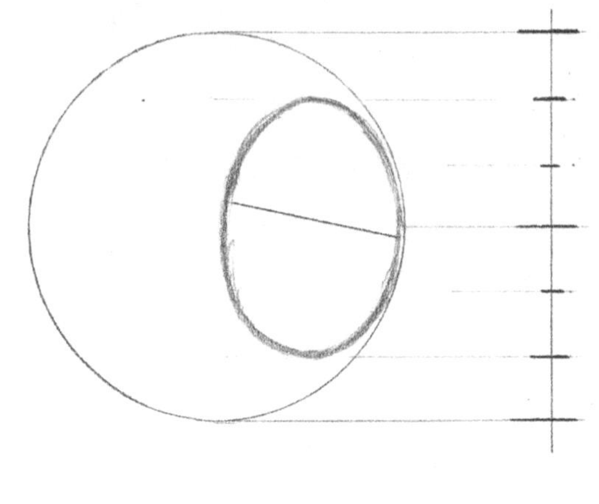

Now, continue drawing this line to the front. Make sure it is still curved and not straight because the face is not flat. The next step is to do the same on the bottom of the oval. Repeat the same procedure, drawing a curve from the oval to the front plane. This will represent the bottom of the nose. Then, measure the distance from the first curve to the second curve, as that will be the distance to the chin. Draw a mark there to keep track of this.

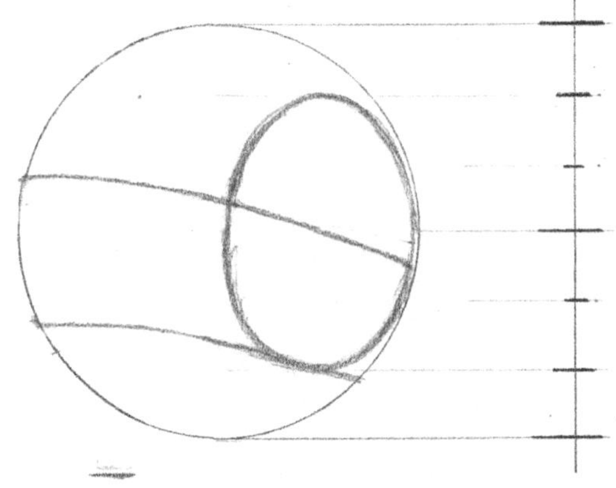

Next, draw a vertical line across the horizontal line on the oval. This will be the guide for the jawline. Try to observe a picture of a head from his angle; you'll notice how the jaw is formed. It usually starts at the middle of the two horizontal lines going down the line of the chin. The same can be seen on the other side, where it starts from the oval's center line down to the chin line.

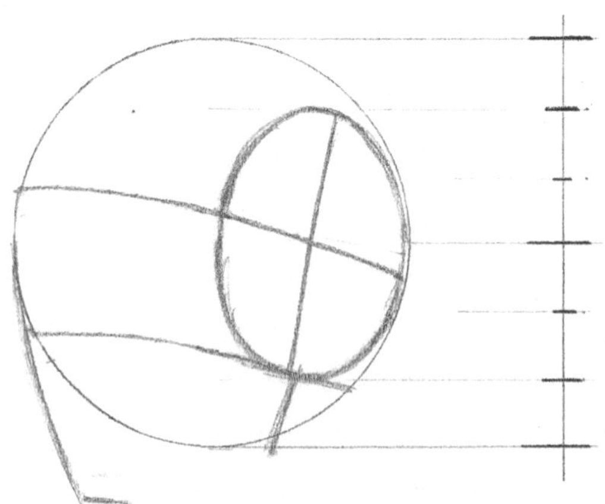

Complete the jaw on the other side. Always keep in mind that the structure of the jaw and the whole face is different for everyone. Then, to complete the side plane, draw a curve starting from the middle of the oval to the corner of the chin line.

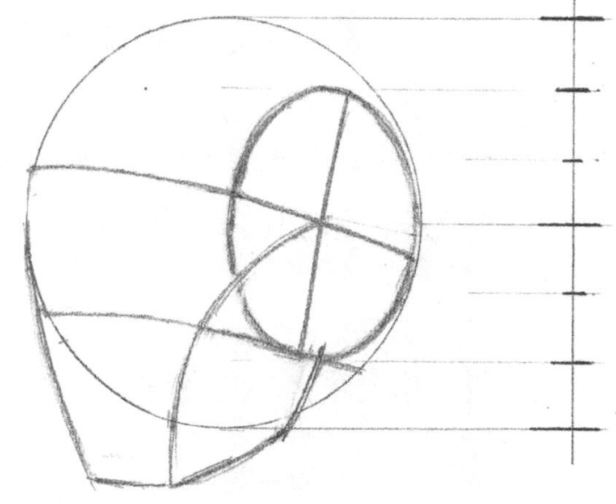

The next step is to find the center of the front plane. It doesn't have to be the middle of the circle because we are not referring to the center of the sphere, but rather the front face. Then, draw the neck. Try to base the neck on some reference with this particular angle.

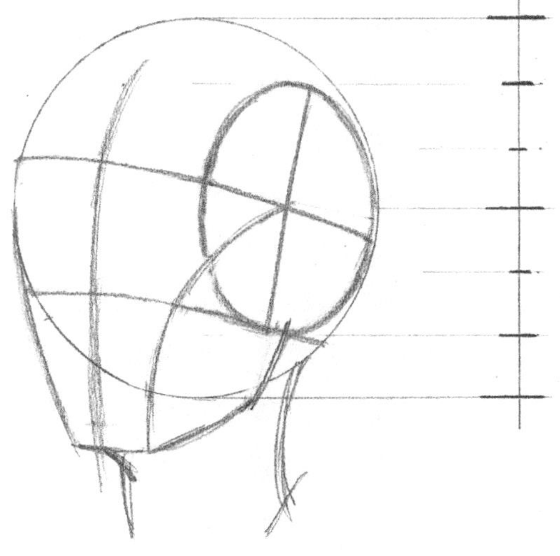

For the final part, work on the details. This is not an easy step, and it takes time to master doing it. One helpful tip is to observe and study references on the web or in books. I suggest that, if you want to learn a certain angle, you should use this technique and also study some references. That way, you'll understand this technique better.

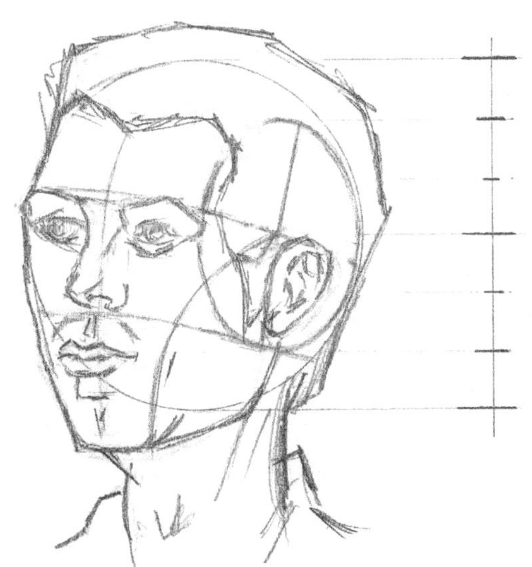

Head Drawing: Angle I

A different approach to head angles is a challenging thing for most people, but the Loomis method will help you get through this phase. Let's begin with this guide.

This will be the typical guide for some angles. Draw a circle that has an oval on its side. Then draw an axis on the oval that is inside the circle. The next step is to draw the front part of the face. To do this, make a straight line on the surface and then a horizontal line, that is slightly angled, to form a perspective.

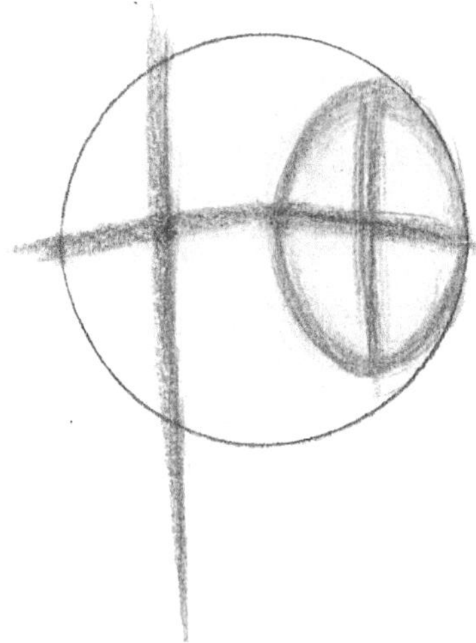

If you want a face that is looking upwards, tilt the guide upwards and make sure to bring the oval or the side plane down to have a view of the top of the head.

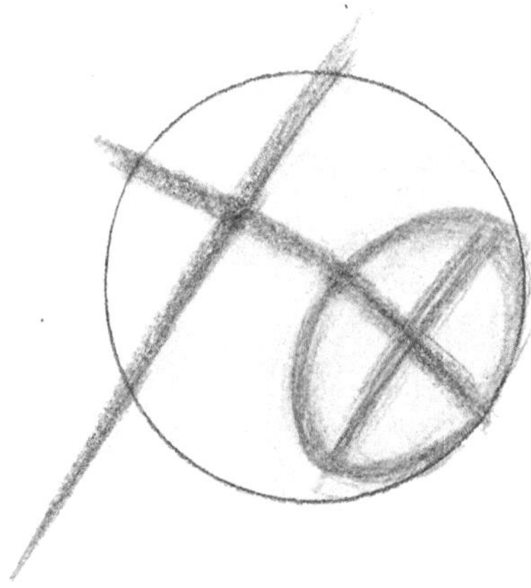

If you want a downward-tilted face, tilt the front plane at a downward angle together with the side plane. This angle will show more of the bottom angles.

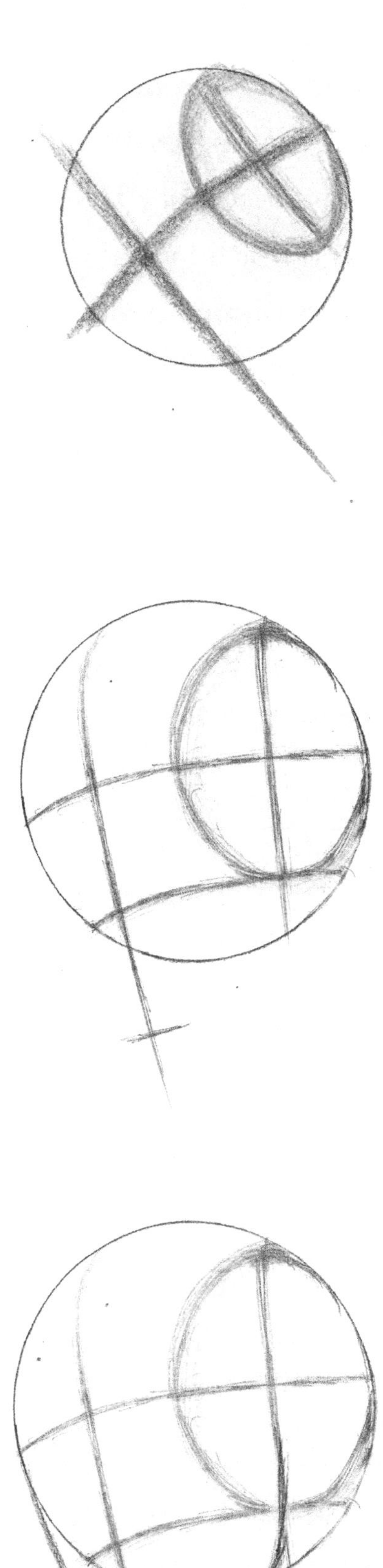

For this particular angle that we are going to do, I chose a slightly downward-tilted head. The method is the same; do the front and side plane, then divide the vertical line in 3. These lines will be the basis for the eyes, nose, lips, and chin. Make sure that the guidelines on the front plane are curvy, because the face is not flat.

Now, carefully define the jaw. Start from the left side's middle to the chin. This will be the cheeks on the other side of the head. Then, from the side plane, the center line of the axis will be the starting line of the jaw, down to the chin line. You may choose how to draw the jaw. As you can see, the head is more defined now.

Now, because the head is defined, try drawing the neck. Although this is not expressly necessary for beginners, there's no harm in learning it. Try observing photos and actual human faces to have a deeper understanding of it.

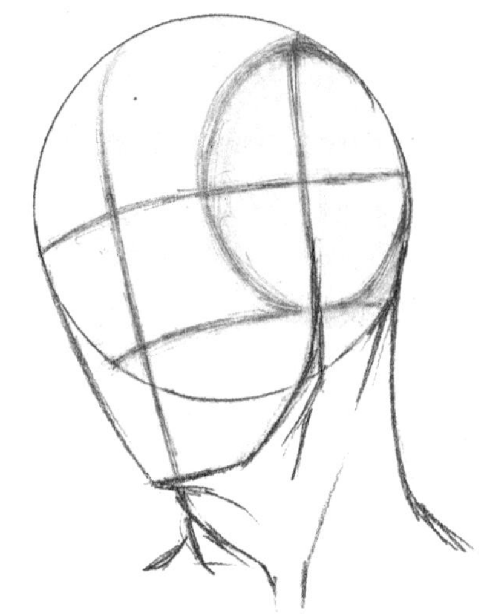

After defining the neck, do not forget about the ears. They sit in the middle of the eye and nose guideline. Then draw the hair. The hair is usually above the sphere guideline. If you draw the hair below this, it will look strange.

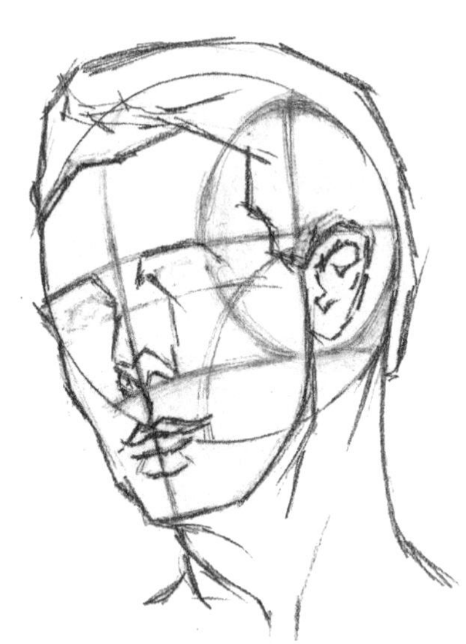

When filling up the face, getting every detail right will be the hardest part. Learning to block the shapes of the face and then using that as a guideline will be the most helpful thing to practice for drawing facial features at an uncommon angle.

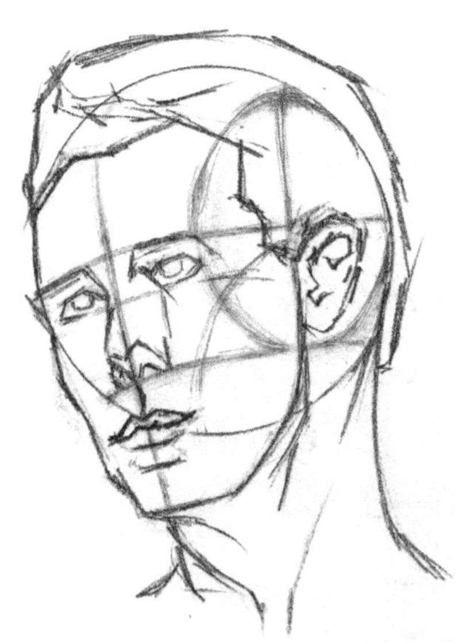

Head Drawing: Angle II

For another extreme angle approach, we are going to try to draw a head looking slightly downward while on a ¾ angle. Let's try it out!

We always start with the ball sketch. Now, where do we place the side plane and how do we chop it off? Since the head we are trying to draw is a bit tilted downward but still facing the front, we will see less of that circle and, instead, a narrow, tilted, oval plane.

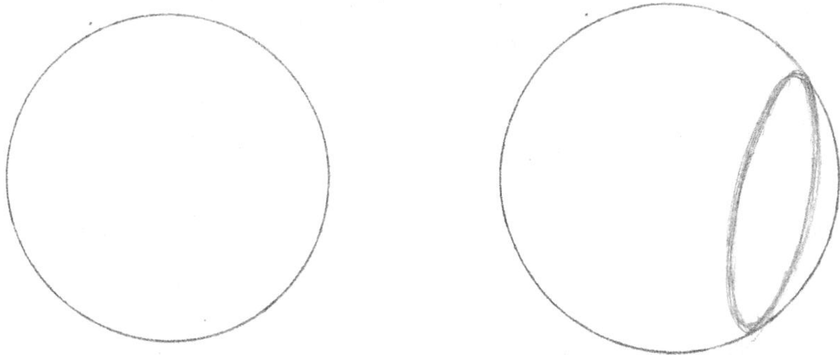

On the other side, we will need to chop off a little bit as well. We will draw a partial oval only because we can't see the back. Then, on the side plane, try to find the middle and draw a line. The line will be facing a bit downwards, as that is how the whole head is positioned.

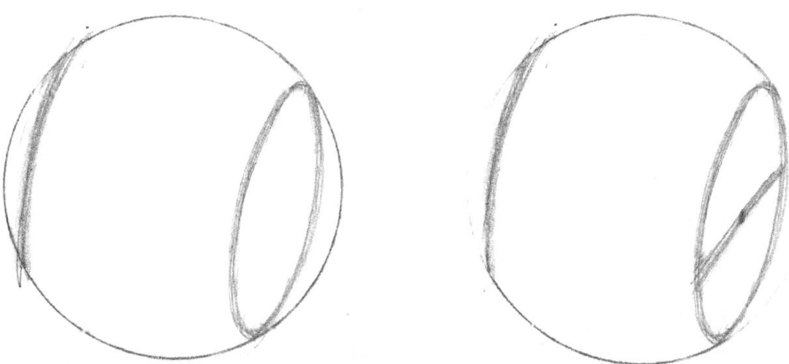

Then, from the line on the side plane, continue to draw a horizontal line in front. It should seem like it is wrapping around the sphere. The next step is to draw a vertical line on the side plane from its center. Thereafter, do the same from our imaginary sphere. Try to find the center and wrap the vertical line around it. That will serve as the center of the head.

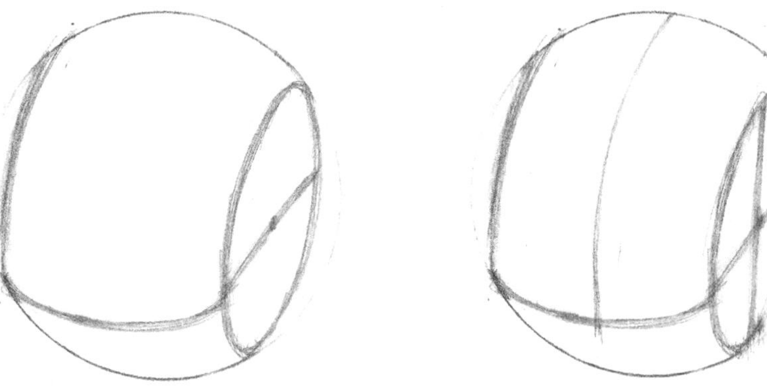

Next, try to draw another semi-curved horizontal line below the first one. This will serve as the guideline for the nose. Then, draw another similar line below that line we just drew, which makes a total of 3 guidelines for the facial features. From the second line on the left side, try to draw the shape of the jaw. Keep in mind that everyone's jaw shape is different and unique. For this example, we are trying to imitate a typical male's jaw, hence the sharp edge. Do the same on the right side, but this time, start defining the jaw at the bottom of the side plane circle. Make those jaw guidelines meet in the third line, which is the guideline for the chin. Now, draw another semi-curved horizontal line on top of the side plane circle up to the other side, this is where the hairline will be.

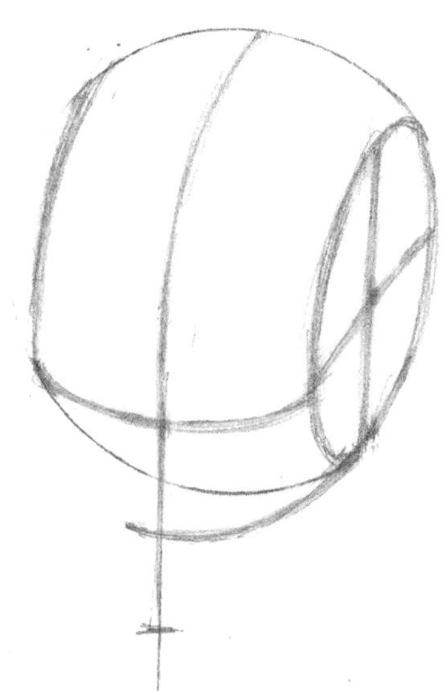

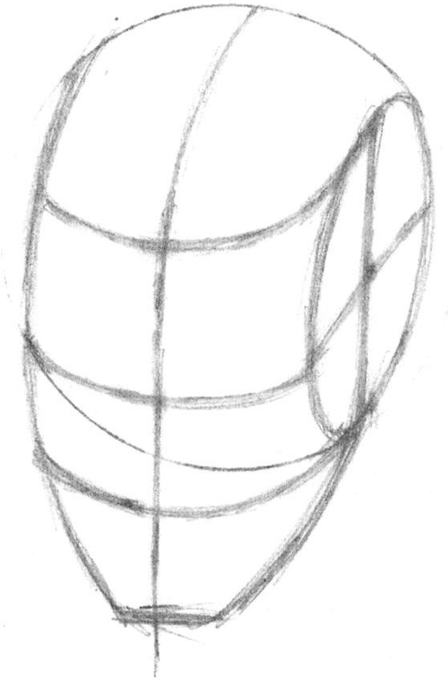

For the final part, we are going to draw another curved line that comes from the top of the side plane circle up to the bottom of the chin. This will define the side plane much better. For this exercise, I recommend using a reference photo to better understand the facial structure.

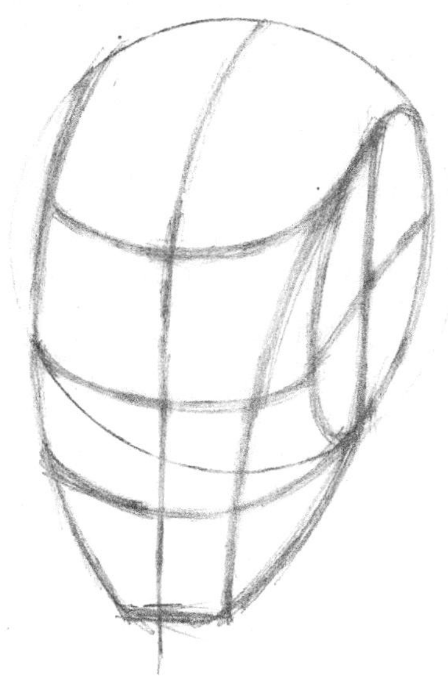 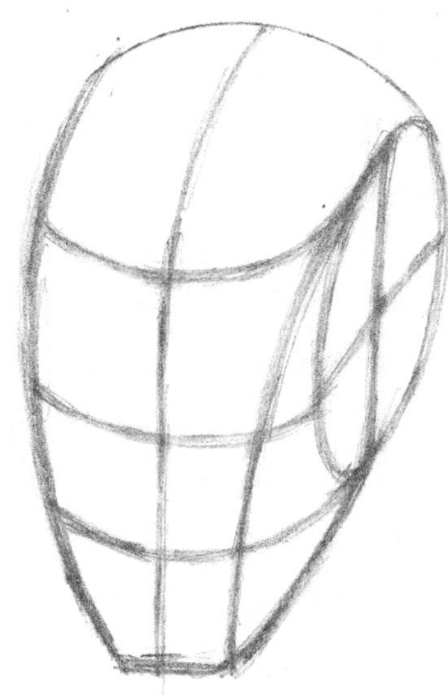

Head Drawing: Different Angles

There are many different head angles that can be drawn using the Loomis method. Almost all angles of the head are possible through this method. On this page, I will show you few more examples of head angles that you can practice on your own.

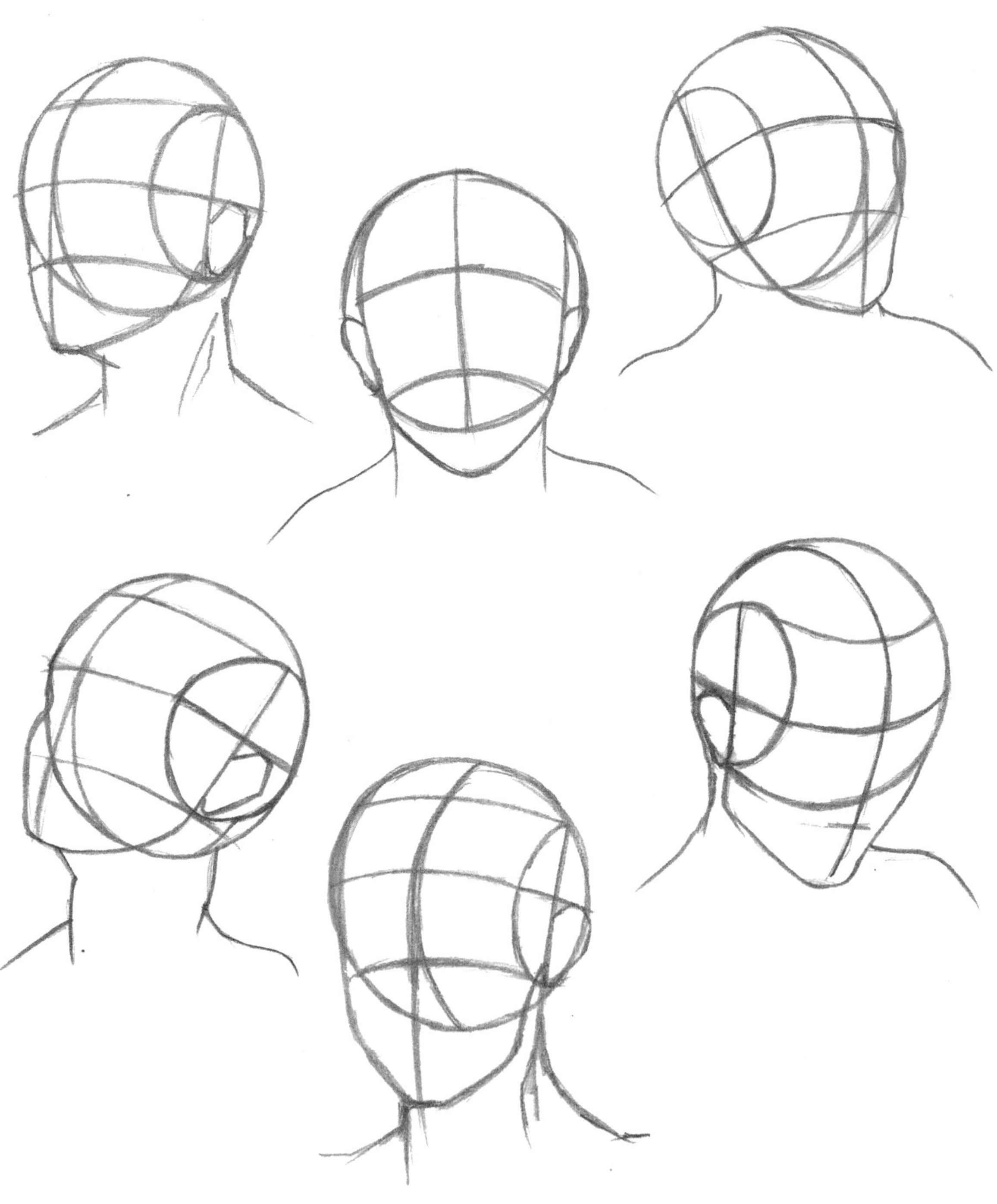

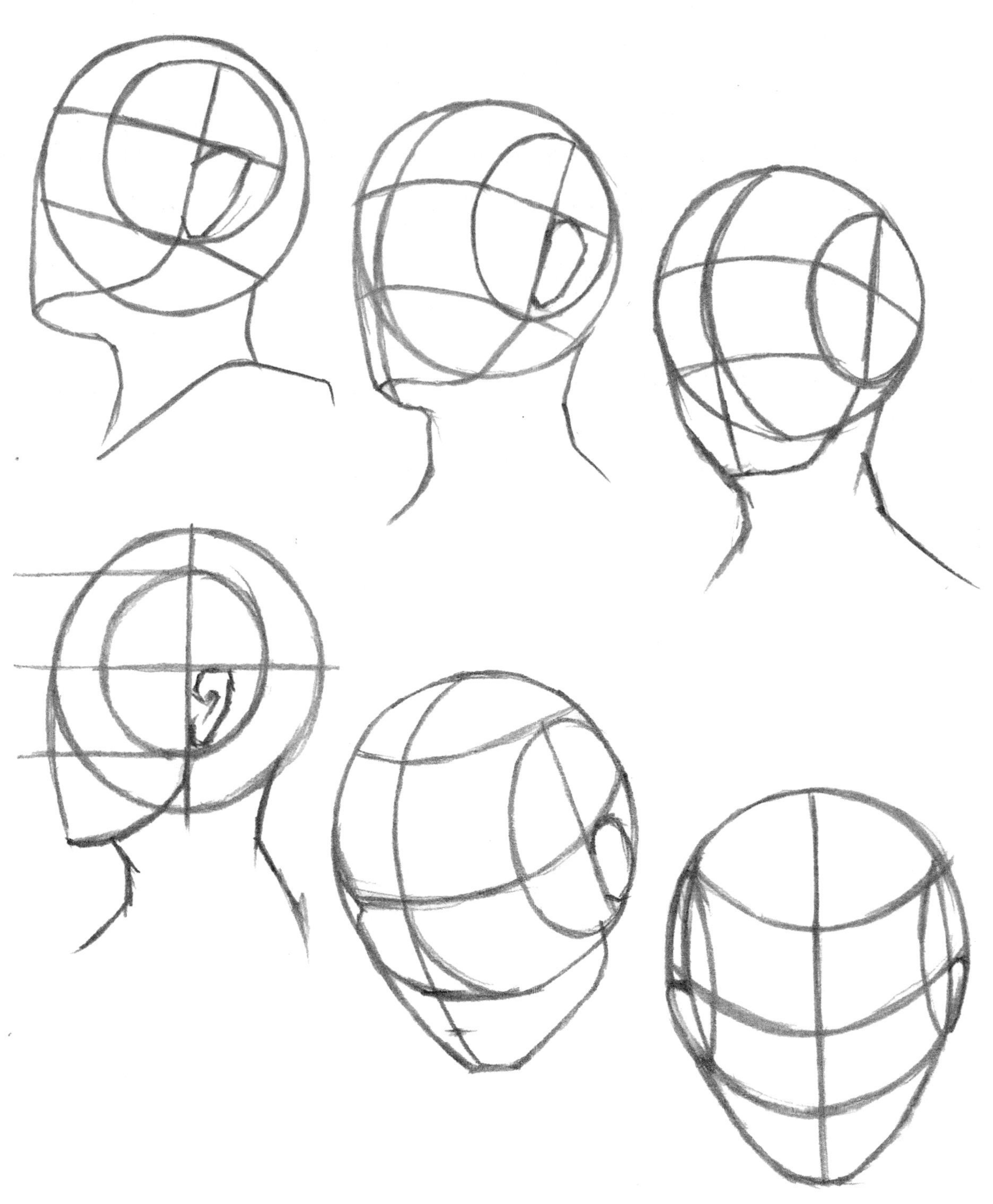

How to Draw a Portrait

Now, using all the methods and techniques we've discussed, we are going to draw a complete portrait from the very beginning. Now let's start.

As always, everything starts with a circle. Don't worry too much if it's not perfect. Keep in mind that this is a mere guide.

The next step is to do the face guidelines. Since this angle we are doing is a bit tilted on the left side, we are going to find the center of it. Since, at this angle, the other side is not visible, we only have the right-side plane to work with.

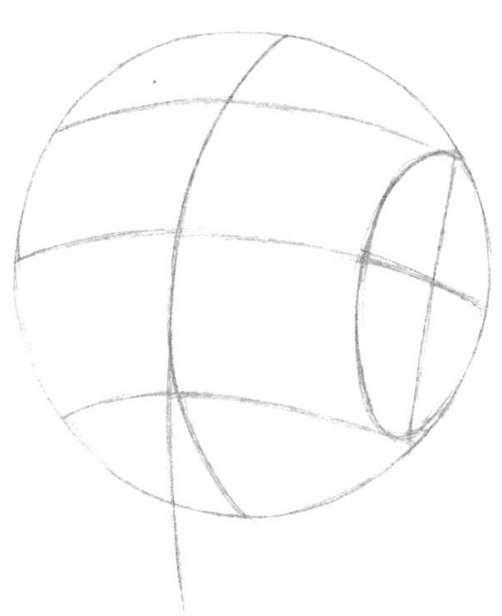

After drawing the guidelines for the facial features, we will draw the shape of the jaw, ears, and neck. As for the face, you can see that we did not take up the whole circle on the left side.

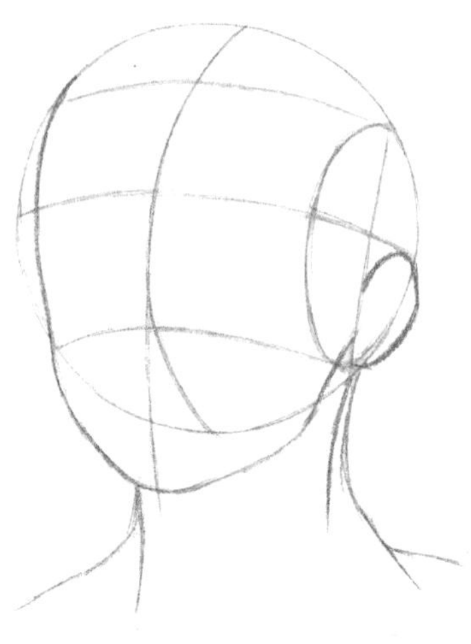

We then slightly erased the pencil drawing just enough to see the outlines. Then, we locate the main guides for every feature. We apply the same rules. For instance, the vertical length of one eye is the same as the distance between them. The only difference is that this portrait will need minor adjustments since the head is a bit tilted on the side. You will then be able to get the guides for the nose and lips when you divide half of the face into 3.

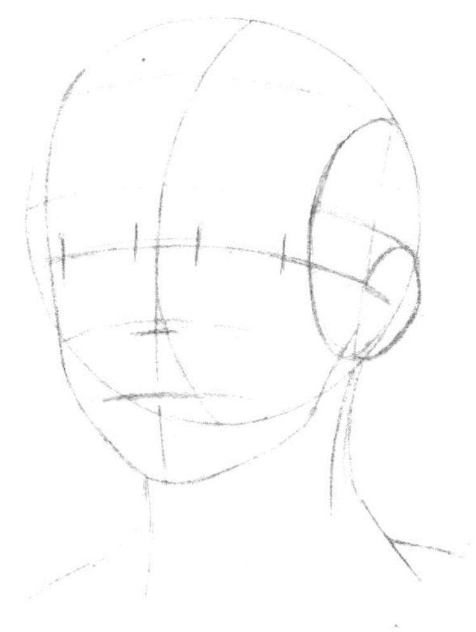

The next step is to define the eyes. Drawing a concave and convex (or, more simply, a pear shape) with a circle on the inside is what makes an eye.

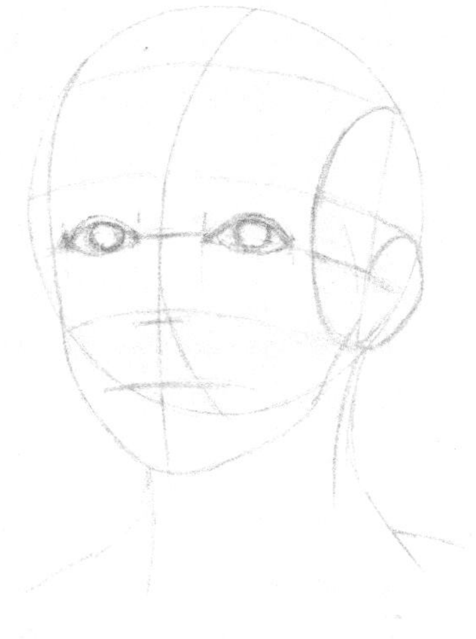

Next, we define the nose and lips. As for the nose, we won't be able to see the nostril on the other side. This is how it looks when tilted. The lips will also be asymmetrical from this angle.

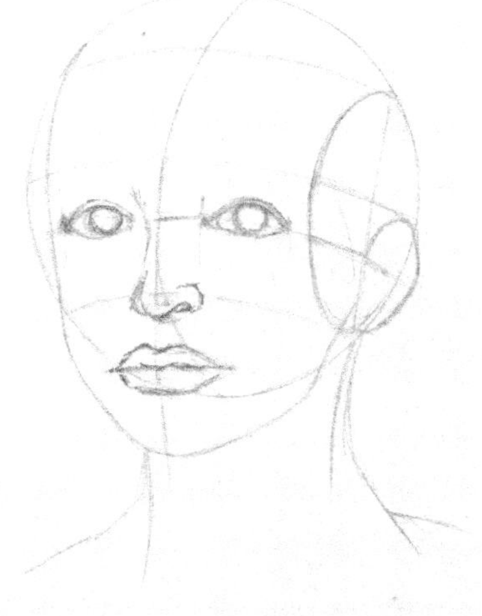

The eyebrows are just under 1cm above the eyes, but all this can vary since everyone has unique features. For the outline of the hair, you are free to decide how'd you like it to be. Just make sure that the outer part of the hair is above our circle guide.

We are about to do the shading, so you must erase the first guidelines carefully. Then, for the main outlines, slightly erase them so they appear faded.

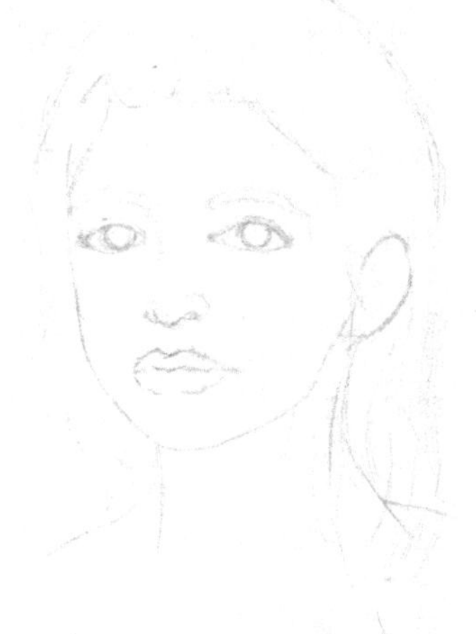

In shading, always do the eyes first, because they are the center of the subject, and everything else will follow. Mindfully draw the outlines of the eyes first before shading the irises. The shading of the iris, depending on the light, is usually darker above and lighter below.

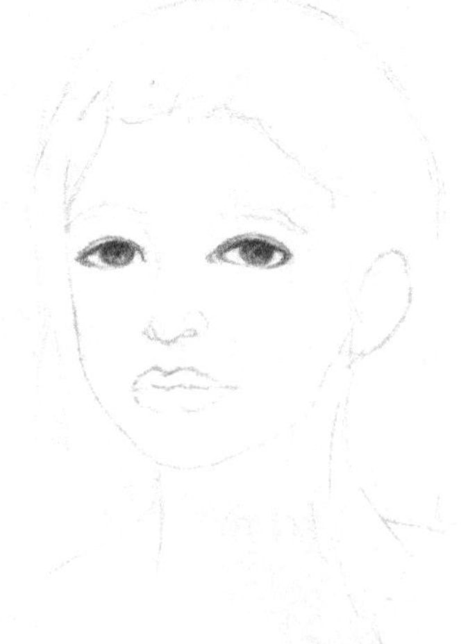

After outlining the eyes, shade them using a blending stump. Make sure that the white of the eyeball is still clean to make it more realistic. Also, do not shade all the creases of the eyes. Slowly shade the nose, remembering that the only dark parts of the nose are the nostrils and tip. The bridge is formed through shading. Then, slowly build up the outline of the lips.

The next step is to slowly build up the shape of the nose by blending. Remember to use blending alone and no outlines. Then, after doing the outline for lips, add shading to them as well. The line that makes the division of the lips is the darkest area, and the surrounding it will get progressively lighter to create the illusion of embossed lips. For the eyebrows, do the outline first - a stroke in an outward direction.

Now that all the features have been partially built up, use the excess graphite or charcoal from the blending stump to blend the skin of the face, starting, as always, with the eyes, eyebrows, nose, and lips. Always make sure to leave clean the highlighted parts of the face.

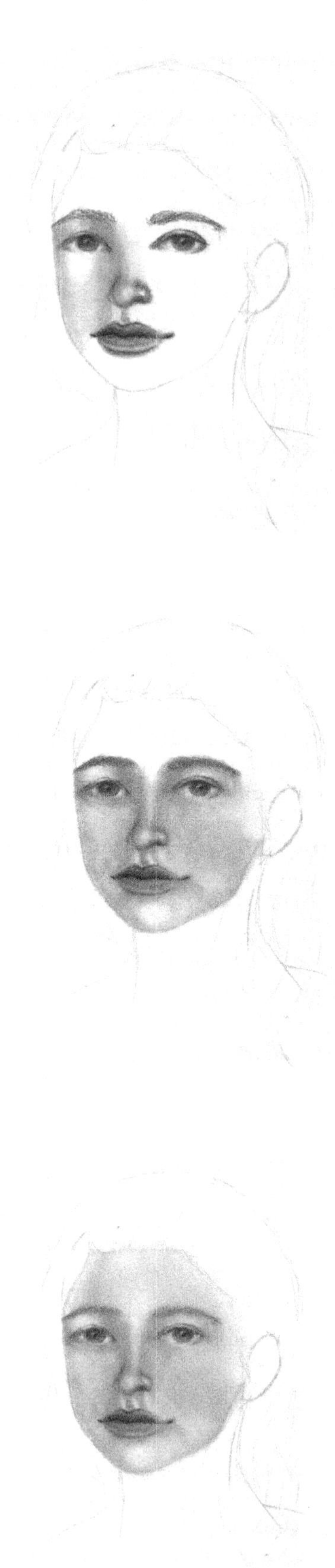

Do the same for the whole face when it comes to blending. As you may have noticed, the highlighted area is the part where the bone structure is visible. This creates a sense of texture and shape for the face. Next, blend the eyebrows using a blending stamp in an outward direction again.

The forehead doesn't need much highlighting, but it is the lightest shade on the face. This always depends, however, on how you'd like the subject to look. As for the sample drawing, the lighting on the face is pointed towards the forehead.

When you are satisfied with the shading on the face, the next step is to finalize the shading using the kneaded eraser. Tap gently on the cheekbone, the tip of the nose, and some areas in the eyes and chin as well. Then, darken the facial features. Do not overdo the outlining, or else the portrait will look cartoonish rather than realistic.

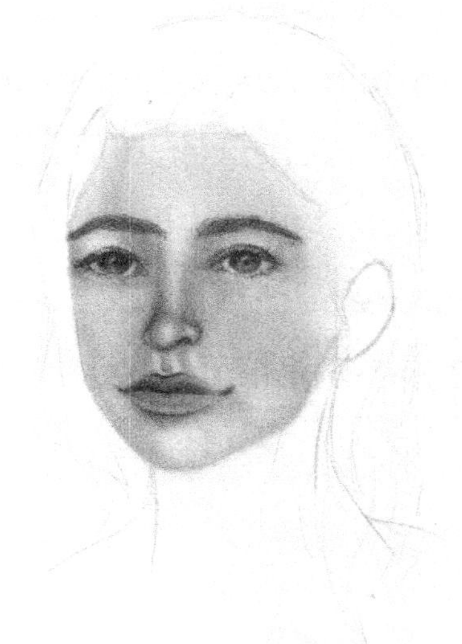

The next step is to outline the hair. Do not be scared if you feel like you've made it darker, as this won't matter later on. Also, draw the eyelashes. They should be a bit darker than the shade you used for the skin.

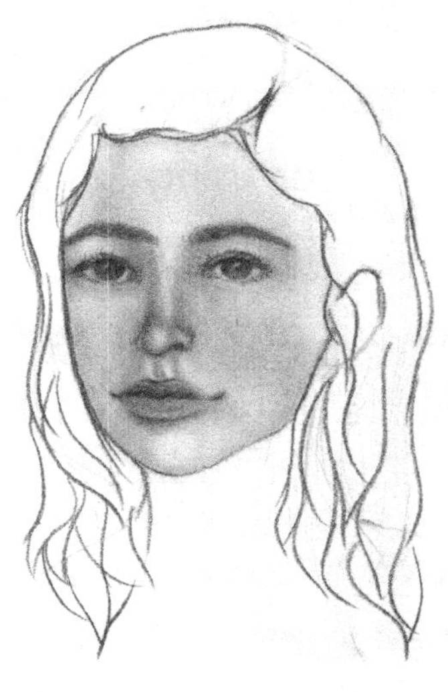

Next, for the hair, do the inner outlines and shade the whole thing. Do not worry too much about this, as if it doesn't look right at the moment, trust me, it will later. Just make sure that, since this shade is darker than what is used on the face, it doesn't create dust on the face or leave marks, because these are hard to remove and erase.

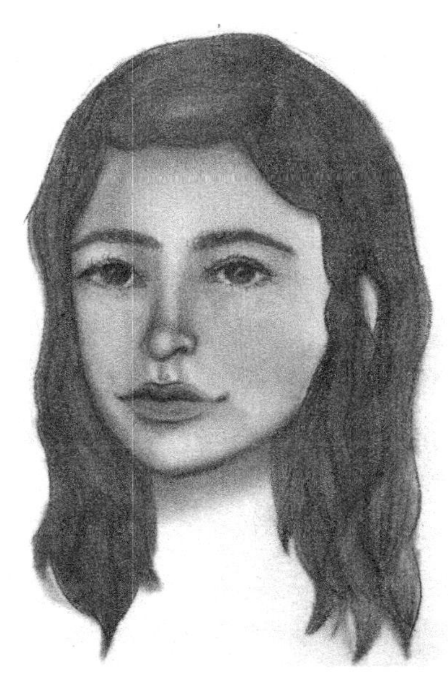

Now, using the kneaded eraser, shape it to have a thin edge. This is what you'll use for the hair strands. Stroke the eraser base along the flow of the hair. Do this repeatedly but not to the point that the whole thing is erased.

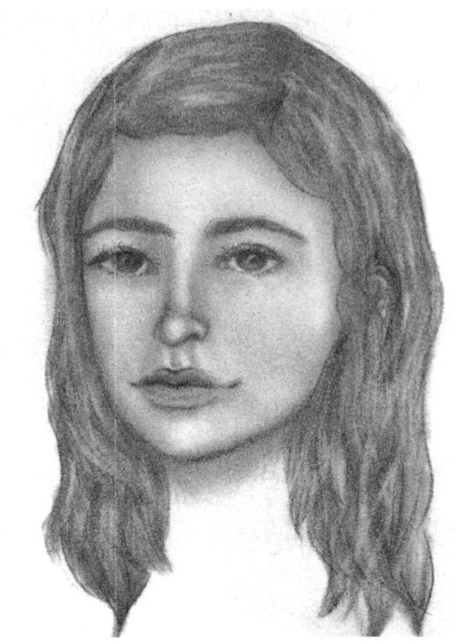

For the last step, finalize everything. For the hair, after using the kneaded eraser for the highlights, use a rubber eraser with a sharp edge to make the final highlights. This is only for the part where the light hits most on the hair. Do not do this on the whole hair area, or it will lose the illusion of volume.

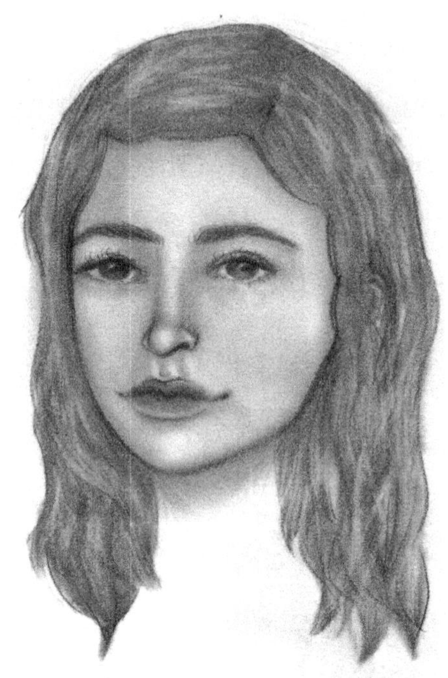

Keep in mind that this is not always the methodology for drawing a portrait - this is merely a guide to help you get started. Try to find more ways and explore more options. Do not limit yourself in doing what is instructed in this book alone. As cliché as it may sound, practice makes progress.

Conclusion

Congratulations! You have reached the end of our guide. It means that you now possess the potential to create a portrait. It is not easy at first, but as they say, practice makes perfect!

Remember these three main ingredients to help you get started: Consistency, Patience, and Enthusiasm. When something goes wrong, don't freak out; just refer to our instructions and restart accordingly.

Let's recall the essential steps: First, learn the different shading techniques, then understand the light and drawing accuracy. Second, discover the importance of line weight and holding a pencil. Lastly, understand the common shading mistakes, blending, and drawing tips and tricks.

Once you have mastered these methods, you can eventually begin developing your own approaches. You might be amazed by what you can think of!

If you enjoy drawing, you will eventually be able to see your development, and wonderful drawings will start to appear. Thank you for purchasing our book!

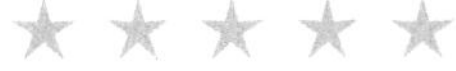

Thank you for buying our book!

If you find this guidebook fun and useful, we would be very grateful if you post a short review on Amazon! Your support does make a difference and we read every review personally.

If you would like to leave a review, just head on over to this book's Amazon page and click "Write a customer review."

Thank you for your support!

Made in the USA
Las Vegas, NV
08 November 2023